21 CENTURY NEWTECHNOLOGY INDUSTRY DEVELOPMENT

JOHN LOK

ISBN 979-888591486-4

Contents

Preface

I write this book aims to give my opinion to explain how computer product organization ought achieve to implement effective marketing strategy.

In first chapter, I shall give reasons to explain how to develop future computer market. I shall indicate what factors will influence computer consumers' laptop purchases behavior as well as explain whether culture factor can influence computer consumer choice behavior. Also, I shall indicatw what service will be future computer related service need market.

In second chapter , I shall indicate whether artificial intelligence will be the best manufacture tool to manufacture any kinds of laptops or desktops in any computer organizations. Does (AI) technology is the best manufacture tools to help anycomputer factories to manufacture any desktops or laptops in order to achieve the most efficient manufacture performance. The only solution for raising productivity and efficiency, who are losing out in the race is investment in all its forms, in both equipment and people. This analysis will be of interest to all those faced with economic decisions: engineers, managers, scientists and administrators as well as economists need to learn how to use technology to solve low efficiency and low productivity challenges in computer factory manufacture environment. As such, it obeys the rules of systems, which include time, information and energy. It also requires an appreciation that technological innovations to machine tools and computers have always been a part of the economic process, and can't be treated as variable factor, some kind of analytical optional extra. I shall explain why and how artificial intelligence will be the best manufacture tools to be used to manufacture any kinds of laptops or desktops in computer manufacture factories.

In chapter three, I shall indicate how computer related service, internet market development tend. Nowadays, internet is one kind of popular technological tool to be used by us. Usually, we shall apply internet for entertainment aspect, such as watching movie, listening music or students will apply internet to gather any data for learning aspect, or we shall apply internet for any information search aspect. Thus, in general, human will apply internet for these both aspects nowadays. However, I shall explain future internet will be used for these both unpredictable or undiscovered actual function aspect, they include business function and online working function both aspects. Moreover, it will imply to be used as soon future in out this century. In this chapter, I shall indicate reasons to explain that why and how internet will be applied to these both functions in popular possible.

Readers can make critical mind to judge whether my view point is correct and it can be occurred from online working and online business to replace our traditional office working model and traditional store business model for future internet function actual development trend.

In chapter four, I shall explain nowadays, on the one hand, technology can bring beneficial positive impact to influence our life. e.g. automate manual driving vehicles, 3D product copying printer invention, advance medical equipment invention, space exploration fast speed shuttles or sky rockets invention etc. different advance technological equipment invention which can raise our standard of living quality and to pursue the aims of human further technological development. However, on the other hand, I also believe technology can bring negative impact to threaten our life in possible, if some scientists and/or these technological products manufacturers only consider themselves benefits to apply any these advanced technological invention to sell to any countries for weapon tools to help them to win competitive effort to achieve these countries can dominate or manage or control other pace countries pursuit.

In my this chapter, I shall give my opinions to explain why I believe technology can be applied to threat our life safety. I write this book aims to let scientists and these technological product manufacturer and the ambitious and dominant countries' leaders to consider that they have responsibilities to apply these technological products to bring any benefits to satisfy human's needs or enjoyment. Thus, any further scientific inventions ought only aim to be contributed to satisfy human's beneficial needs, they ought not to be manufactured to help any ambitious countries' leaders to raise their effort to apply these technological products to attack or dominate their enemy to encourage wars in our earth.I shall concentrate on explaining these several technological invention aspects to let scientists to consider their further scientific inventions why will cause negative impact to threaten human's life safety if their pursuits are immoral to achieve their profit earning intention only from the ambitious countries' leaders. These important and influential scientific inventions include that, such as artificial intelligence, biochemistry medical research, nuclear energy invention, space exploration speed and alien communication pursuit technological invention.

Finally, in my this chapter, I shall give my opinions to attempt to explain why scientists ought consider these questions why their immoral intentions or behaviors will threaten human's life safety by these new technological inventions as below:Can human become artificial intelligent machines' servants? Can biochemistry healthy research be applied to become any diseases weapons to attack ourselves? Can nuclear invention be applied to become different kind of nuclear bomb weapons to attack ourselves and to cause wars occurrence? Is any space exploration expenditures be valueless or waste to carry on any unpredictable confident space exploration activities, such as Mar exploration or noon exploration etc.? Will space technology become technological weapons to be applied to attack ourselves or to encourage space wars? Ought scientists need to invent different technologies weapons to predict when space stones will fly to crash our earth to cause human death and to decide to apply what kind of technological weapons to attack the space stones, to replace to spend time and expenditure to invent any telecommunication tools to communicate with alien? All above technology will be concerned to how human applies computer technology to develop our teachnology market to let human to use. In final chapter, I shall indiate what factors can influence Canada future social general computer industry consumer market. My research main aim to apply behavioral economy methods to predict what consumption model is Canadian chooses to buy high technology computer products or use any computer technological related services social attitude in general. What can macro or micro economic factors influence Canadian have consumption desires to plan to use computer products or computer related technological serice in social. In this chapter, I shall also apply macro or micro economic methods to predict what general future Canadian computer technological product or service need in Canada society. How to improve Canada economic development and give recommendations how to sell computer products or computer related provide services to attract Canadian to consume more easily from Canadian life habitual view point analysis.

I write this book concerns to research whether computer industry will bring what negative influences will be caused to impact human quality of standard to be poor or better. Although, computer technology can rise productivity or performance to any entrepreneurs. But, computer technology can also bring negative impact to influence our life. Whether can it influence student learning abilities to be poorer? How can it bring negative impact to influence our life, e.g. poorer to influence student learning? I shall analyze it's negative impacts to our life on technological labor market, internet learning and computer entertainment and smart phone three kinds of technological aspects.

It is suitable to any readers who have interest to research what factors will cause computer technology development to bring negative or positive impact to cause human to get any disadvantages or advantages in our nowadays societies as well as how we can avoid to be influenced worse quality of life by computer negative influences. This book is suitable to any readers who have interest to predict how future computer industry will develop to be influenced and computer businessmen can predict or dominate to build better consumer behavior in global computer consumption market.

Prologue

Table Of contents

- The relationship between the production of factor and technological innovation.

What is the relationship between the process of technological innovation and the production of factor?

What is the process of technological innovation in the factor of production?

How to response times in technological innovation?

Why technological innovation will be one factor of production to computer technological manufacture industry.

How can external and internal factors affect the product and business process innovation?

What is production of factor knowledge economy

Production of factor internal technical skill

Reference

Chapter 3

Internet market development trend

- What is Internet entertainment function p.55-67
- What is Internet learning function p.68-78
- What is internet for searching information function p.79-89
- What is internet for online office Function p.90-101
- What is internet for ecommerce Function p.102-112

Chapter 4

Computer technology related service consumer negtive emotion factors

- Technology negative influence reasons

Six key forces or " Drivers of change" impact on future internet development

- Future trend of mobile and internet development
- Digital Pollution prediction tool development

How can we use the internet tool to predict pollution to improve health

How does internet predict air pollution

Chapter 5

Factors influence Canada computer market development

- Canada and Norway Similar

behavioral consumption model p.162-180

- Living standard, productivity and

competitiveness to international

comparison factor

- Innovation policy factor influences Canadian

behavioral consumption model

- Immigrant economic and social factor influences Canadian consumption model changes

High impact firms accelerate Canadian

competitiveness influence technological product

consumer behavioal changes

Implementing Canada's rural development policy in a knowledge-driven economic consumption behaviors.

How can greening of the Canadian economy to influence businesses' behavioral changes

Increase productivity growth influences to increase social consumption in Canada

How growth strategy influences

Canadian consumption model changes

CHAPTER ONE

Computer Consumer Behavior

Why China's computer manufacturing and product development industry will be global leader to compete US computer dominant market.

Nowadays, China's computer industry is the largetest hardware producer production and experts is dominated by Taiwanese firms. It is also the second largest personal computer (pc) market and domestic pc companies are top three sellers in global computer manufacturing and product development market. Forx example, Lenovo buys BM pc business in 2004 year. It implies US, IBM pc manufacturing leader can not dominate global computer market in possible in the future.

Reed Electronic Research, Yearbook Of World Electronic Data (2003) indicated that the leading computer producing countries of hardware production in US $millions and share share of total gogal production: The world region US was the global rank number one. In 1995 year, US had US $76,284 value, market value 26.5%. Then in 2000 year, US had increased up to US $ 90, 430 value, market share 24%. Till to 2003 year, US had fallen down to US $ 69,102 value, market share 21.7%. However, US hardware production was still the global rank number one , although its hardware production value had been falling down. But, the following second rank country, Japan and the third rank country, Singapore and the fourth rank country, Taiwan and the fifth rank county China which hardware production value could not exceed US till to 2003 year. However, although China had the lowest hardware production value US $5,600 to compare to among of these countries in 1995 year, but China had increased the value to US $65,000 and market share to 20.5%. Otherwise, Japan, Singapore and Taiwan value and market share had surprisingly fallen down below than China value in 2003 year. Thus, it seemed that China will be a potential country to compete US hardware production industry after 2003 year.

Reed Electronic Research, Year book Of World Electronic Data (2003) also showed that these computer companies of China had these % of market share : Beijing Founder had 9.9%, Tsinghua Tongtang had 7.8%, dell had 7.2 % , IBM had 5.1% , HP had 4.8% of market share. Thus, it also seemed that China some computer companies will have impotant large market share percentage in global pc sale market. In the future, global hardware production and pc sale industry. China and Taiwan both countries will be one pc manufacturing and design and sale partner. The reason is that China and Taiwan had been the number one rank of markers of notebook pcs, motherboards, scanners, keyboards, add-on card optical drives, monitors and some network equipment etc. pc (personal computer) relative computer function products. It seems that these both countries had co-operated to research any computer relative products to sell to global computer market. They are also the original design manufacturers (DDMS) develop and manufacture over half the world's notebook pcs as well as their customers include all major branded pc vendors (OEMS).

Taiwan Minstry Of Economic Affairs (2003) indicated Taiwan's top notebook ODMS include: In 2003 year volume (thousands) Quanta had $8,500 sale volume thousands , for example, Quanta major OEM partners include Gateway, Dell, HP, IBM, Apple , Sharp, Sony, Fujitsu-Siemens (F/S). Compal had $6,000 sale volume (thousands) , Compal major OEM partners include Dell, HP, F/S, Toshiba, Acer. Thus, it also implied Taiwan had many small size and non famous brand of computer companies which choose to

co-operate to be partners with some global large size and famous brand of computer companies to raise competitive effort in global computer market, such as Dell, IBM, HP, Gatway, Apple etc.
Thus, the future trend of computer new product manufacturing development will shift from US to Taiwan and SE Asia, then to China. However, what kind of knowledge work factors will be needed to China and Taiwan . In general, notebook manufacturing stages will include: The first process is design stage, it includes concept design, such as analyze need, create concept and set brand image as well as product planning, such as business case, specifications, industrial design and sourcing strategy. The second process is development stage, it includes design review steps, such as design review, such as mock-ups, electrical test as well as prototype build, such as commercial samples, integrated system test as well as pilot production, such as production process design, pilot. Final process is production stage, it includes mass production, such as ramp-up, volume production, production testing and global distribution as well as sustaining support, such as speed bump, component replacement, technical support and warranty support. Thus, I believe that China and Taiwan must own thee knowledge work skillful of computer design and development professionals who can assist these two countries how to innovate their future computer development to change global traditional computer model to be renew and innovate computer model in the future.
Due to computer industry's stages of development and manufacturing are closely linked , need manufacturability , testing of sample products, concept design and product planning stay together in lead markets and branded vendors, design and development can be separated organizationally and geographically. Thus, China and Taiwan choose to co-operate to exchange their different skill, such as either China has own more concept design and product planning skill or more development skill or more production skill. Then, China will choose either one of the most beneficial comparative advantage among of them. To bring this one of the most beneficial co-operative advantage to attract Taiwan to

choose either one of the beneficial comparative advantage of skill, such as either design or development or producton to already co-operate to compete the Western developed country US together. Thus, US won't be the global computer industry development leader if both US country famous and large employee number computer companies, such as IBM and Apple which choose to outsource their pc design and development and production skill to China and Taiwan both countries to help them to develop global computer design and development and production skill to be upgraded. Thus, I feel these both countries will plan how to co-operate to compete US to win the global computer industry leader position in the future.

Factors influence consumers' laptop purchases.

In the future, instead of global computer manufacters need to consider the design, development and production processes, who also need to consider what factors can influence consumers' laptop purchases. Because any consumers have much different computer model and brand to choose to make final decision to buy any computers. If the computer manufacturer can predict what factors will be whose weakness(es) to influence global computer consumers to change whose mind or attitude to choose to buy other brands of computers, then it won't lose its many old computer customer numbers and reduces it market share in global computer market share.

Nowadays, in general computer has three kinds to provide to global consumers to choose to buy , such as laptop, notebook computers, desktops. it seems that laptop and notebook computers and desktops will have different factors to influence any consumers to choose to buy any brand of computer products. Thus, computer indsutry can divide three consumer groups, such as (stayers, satisfied switchers and dissatisfied switchers) of a computer company with respect to the factors influencing consumers' laptops or notebook computers or desktops purchases. However, I feel the factors can include such as core technicl features, post purchase services, prices and payment conditions, peripheral specification, physical appearance, value added features and connectivity and mobility seven main factors that are influencing consumers' laptop or notebook computer or desktop purchases in global computer industry market.

Ganesh et al., (2000) indicates the customer base of a company consists of three groups of consumers: stayers, satisfied switchers and dissatisfied switchers. Therefore, the consumers in this study replied to the question about whether the current brand that who were using was their first laptop brand or whether who had switched from a previous laptop brand. As a following question, consumers who had switched were asked to state the reason of why who switched from a previous laptop brand brand to their current brand. The options include overall dissatisfaction from the previous laptop brand and reasons other than dissatisfaction. Thus, computer companies need to know what factors influence either whose prior computer customers why who don't choose repeat to buy its any computer products or whose new potential computer customers why who don't choose to buy its any computer products in the first time choice. Thus, future computer manufacturers need to consider intangible salespeople service attitude or performance, such as salespeople current purchase and post purchase service, e.g. technical repair, model function explanation how to use the computer, instead of tangible product performance, e.g. computer appearance design , function , mobility and internet and document download speed connectivity function. Because salespeople and technicians‘ service performance can be represented to the computer image. If they can provide excellent service to let computer buyers to feel satisfactory, then they can help their computer company employer to build good image. So, staff service performance will be one important factor to influence computer consumers to make the final decision to choose to buy the brand of computer products more easily. Even, one famous brand computer company, such as IBM, Apple, Gateway, these any one of famous brand computer company must not attract any new (the first time) or repeat computer buyers to choose to buy their any kind of computer products , such as laptop, desktop or notebook more easily due to their famous brand. Althoug, these famous computer companies had built good image to let consumers have more confidence to buy any kind of their computer products. But, if these famous computer companies' salepeople or repair technicians can not provide excellent customer service or performance to satisfy their computer buyers' service need, e.g. explaining how to use the new computer, repair post purchase service etc. I believe these famous brands of computer consumers will not have more desire to prefer to chose to buy any one of these famous computer brand's products. Otherwise, if the other less famous computer companies' any kind of laptop, desktop or notebook sale price is higher than the famous brand of computer companies' products sale price, but their salepeople or technicians can provide more excellent service attitude or performance to satisfy their consumers' needs. It is possible that the new or first time computer buyers or repeat computer buyers will still choose to buy their computers. So, the famous or less famous computer brand is not one important factor to influence the computer buyer to decide either to buy the computer or not buy the computer. Otherwise, computer company's salepeople and repair technician whose service performance or attitude will be one important intangible factors to influence any first time (new) or repeat computer consumers to choose to buy any famous or less famous brand of computer company's product, instead of the tangible computer design appearance and reliable function and convenient mobility and long term durability etc. factors influences.

Can culture factor influence the computer consumer choice?

Durmza and Zengin, (2011:53) indicted marketers closely interested in this issue to know the family which changed and renewed in course in time. It provides an advantage for a marketer to know the family structure and its consumption characteristics. Nowadays, consumer behavior is influenced not only by consumer personalities and motivation, but also by the relationships within families. Family is a social group and it can be considered a crucial place in th perception of marketing (Durmaz, Yakup, CELLK, Mucahit and ORUC, Reyhan, (2011).

The consumer buying behaviors examined through an empirical study. Then, it brings this question: Whether cultural factors will influnece the computer consumer choice. Choice and include computer brand choice, computer price choice, computer model choice, computer design choice, laptop or desktop or notebook product choice, new or second-hand old computer choice, the computer of manufacturing country choice, computer package choice etc. So, any consumer will consider to choose any one of these to decide to buy which kind of computer.

Every country computer consumers had different culture to influence their computer shopping choice. I feel culture can be explained how to influence to computer shopping such as: How do the country computer consumers buy and use their computer products habitually ? How do the country computer consumers react to th computer price changes, attractive advertising methods to satisfy whose needs and computer company store interiors? What underlying mechanisms operate to produce any one of the country computer consumers‘ responses? If computer marketers have answers to such these questions, who can make better managerial decisions how to adopt which computer target country (countries) consumers' culture.

Consumer behavior deals with many other issues, for instance (Priest, Carter and Statt, 2013: 19). How do we get information about products? How do we assess alternative products? How do different people choose or use different products? How do we decide on value for money ? How much risk do we take with what products? Who influences our buying decisions and our use of the product? How are brand loyalties formed and changed? For computer industry, it means that how computer consumers get information about computer products, how computer consumers assess alternative notebook, desktop, laptop computer products, how different age, country, culture, sex, student or working people or retired people computer consumers choose or use different kind of computer products, such as notebook, desktop, laptop computer products, how much risk computer consumers take with notebook, desktop, laptop computer products, the computer consumers' buying decisons and their use of the desktop or notebook or laptop computer products will be influenced by whom, e.g. family, friends, teacher, employer, computer salepeople, advertisement marketer etc. , computer company brands how are formed and changed by whom, e.g. computer consumers, computer company competitors, marketers, different countries' culture etc.

Durmaz and Jablonski, (2012:56) also explained culture is the essential character of a society that distinguishes it from other cultural groups. The underlying elements of every culture are the values, language, myths, customs, laws and the artifacts or products that are transmitted from one generation to the next (Lamb, Hair and Deniel, 2011: 371). Culture is the most fundamental determinant of a person's wants and behavior. Whereas, lower creatives are governed by instinct, human behavior is largely learned. The child growing up in a society leans a basic set of values, perceptions, preferences and behaviors through a process of socialization involving the family and other social roles. So, I feel different country have different culture to influence as well as different country computer consumers who have different computer purchase and consume habitually. So, computer manufacturers ought focus on manufacturing the unique need and characteristics to satisfy any country's consumers' needs.

What is my idea about future global computer competition and factors influence computer consumer behavior ?

In conclusion, future computer industry development will trend that computer manufacturers need to consider every country's computer comsumer culture. Because every country computer consumers who will have different computer consumption habitually if who can predict what the country most computer consumers culture, then they can have more confidence to sell their computers to different country markets. Moreover, US computer manufacturers need to consider China and Taiwan computer manufacturing technology because it is possible that these both countries will be its main competitor among different computer manufacuring countries. Because thess both countries will cooperate to research new model of different computers to attract global computer consumers to choose to buy their new model of computer products in the future. Finally, computer manufacturers need to consider salepspeople and repair technicians service performance because computer consumers will consider intangible service performance , instead of tangible computer quality and price and style etc. factors . The main reason is that any computer have chance to be needed to repair and salespeople' skill will influence the computer consumer to make final decision to choose to buy the brand of computer. Thus, these factors will influence global computer development and trend in the future.

● Computer industry related service market development

What kinds of technologies innovation products will impact our future lives.

Europe in the 21 St Century is a technological society, how today technological trends could impact upon society in ways to be fully considered by clients' needs. What technological advancement products which can carry trend with it the promise of saving time, or assisting business or manufacturer industry clients to do more in the same amount of time.

In our clients buying choice view point, who ought hope any technological innovation products which can offer them that the opportunity to do things more efficiently. I shall suppose that technological innovation will be the main factor which can attract future many clients' purchase choice from the owned technological innovation product seller. For example, mobility, resource security , electronic government technological innovation products will be popular trend in future technological innovation product market.

● Autonomous automatic vehicle

Can autonomous vehicles be popular in the future driving market?

Will your child soon be driving you to work? The autonomous vehicles (artificial intelligent vehicles) will change the responsible driver concept. Why does autonomous vehicles will be future popular driving tools?

In fact, autonomous vehicles have these feature characteristics to differ to compare our common traditional driving tools. Their characteristics, such as real-time human control option, advantage of the large amount of high -quality mapping data of possesses to programing travel routes, exploring ways in which autonomous vehicle technology can be integrated with existing parking infrastructure to produce " driverless parking systems" accessible via existing personal electronic devices, e.g. smartphones is demonstrating the use of fully automated road transport systems in Europe and developing guidelines to design and implement such systems.

With some analysts predicting that by 2022 year , there will be around 1.8 billion automotive machine -to-machine connection its is clear that a large amount of data will be generated by vehicle in the future. Thus, this level of communication between automated vehicles should make to possible for such vehicles to navigate to destinations and interact with other vehicles and objects most effectively than a human brain. Moreover, they believe the chance of automatic vehicles‘ highway accidents occurrence will be less than traditional human driving vehicles.

Thus, the increased connectivity required to facilitate automation of vehicles would significantly improve the degree of monitoring of the performance of such vehicles. Individual owners would be able to better maintain and enhance their vehicles with improvements in fuel efficiency and lesser fuel spending and safety. This could also provide further benefits, such as terms of reducing traffic jams, reduced pedestrian exposure to pollution and lower risk of road-traffic and pedestrian incidents occurring, particularly in urban areas.

The rise of autonomous vehicles is also likely to combine with continuing electrification of vehicles as telecommunications software and hardware and further integrated into vehicles. Thus, the rental-orientated and purchase-orientated automatic vehicle business both models will have chance to be raised in future global driving market.

It causes the responsibility tends to lie with human drivers of vehicles will be decreased. A new set of IT skills in addition to a practical ability to drive and operate a more digital type of driving machine as well as it might impact upon existing vehicle users in terms of requiring re-training, particularly those less able to learn. Even, future public transport will have possible to be changed from non-human driving and change to automatic vehicle market will be individual and business both client markets in possible.

In conclusion, to success to sell non manual driving tools. The non manual driving sellers need to know how to solve these two artificial intelligent vehicles innovation questions: Could our future living habits change as a direct segment of changing transport behaviors? Will autonomous transport simply become and essential transportation tools for our homes and workplaces? Thus, if manufacturers want artificial intelligent vehicles sale number increases, which needs to influence future whose clients to accept this kind of non -human driving tools can be satisfy to change their traditional driving living habits for their new habit of non -manual driving method to substitute traditional manual driving tools.

● 3 D printer

Can 3 D printer be popular sale to manufacturing industry clients? What could be the effects to the physical environment and human health of such application 3D printer to copy to manufacture any productions? For example, medical equipment products, car keys, guns, furniture etc. different heavy or light weight manufacturing products.

The benefits to 3 D printer include: less production time, reducing purchase bulk or materials to produce any products, reducing to employ worker number to produce products, workers can learn to use 3D printer to copy to manufacture any products easily, to avoid air or water pollution to pollute working environment to influence worker health and safe production in factories, employers can pay less wages to employ less workers, workers can also raise more efficient during using 3 D printers to manufacture any products.

Thus, in the future 3 D printers can be popular to be used to copy to manufacture for these any products, e.g. jewelry or weapon industry products. In fact, 3 D printer is an additive manufacturing technology for making three- dimensional object, of almost one sharp using a digital model. Such as jewelry manufacturers apply it to copy to manufacture new kind of jewelry, hospitals can apply it to copy to manufacture any new medical equipment, weapon manufacturers can apply it to copy to manufacture any new gun weapons, aerospace or air plan manufacturers can apply it to manufacture new air plane engineering equipment or space exploration equipment or transportation tools. Thus, 3 D printer application will be popular to different aspects of manufacturing industry.

Future expected impacts and development for 3 D printer development. A macro economy level impact of 3 D printing will be considered to manufacturing industry business consumer-based economy and the societal behavioral acceptance in factories and offices manufacturing environment.

However, buying habits as individuals are able to print their own products, in comfort of their own home. Activity would be changed from traditional shopping methods to purchase 3 D printer to copy to manufacture own same products at home. Consumers can also choose how to design to print the product, rather than the manufacturing process itself is what consumers will be paying for and thus these is the potential for a design -lead choice behavior. Manufacturers don't need to buy many materials to manufacture products, they can use 3D printer , such as individual manufacturing machine parts, which could drastically improve their ability to design and manufacture more effective machine and components.

In conclusion, how to sell 3 d printer successfully. 3 D printer sellers need to know what advantages can give to 3 D individual consumption buyer and business buyer to let them to know to aim to let them to accept to change their buying behavior and manufacturing behavior for some products. There are some questions for consumers to attempt to answers:

What will the implications be the level of personal interactions between individuals in society of all of our products were to be manufacturing at home?

How would this change our typical buying habits and what would be the impact on our economy?

Would an increased use of 3D printing technology in the home or factory accelerate this process and what would be the implications for local high streets?

Would economies change being-focused will digital design skills having a greater benefits than traditional manufacturing methods?

If the ability to print everyday items at home becomes a reality , who is society would have the greatest access to such technology?

If a particular demographic section (age, gender, race, income levels can be in factor to influence 3D printer consumer group, e.g. the 3 D printer buyer needs skills to manufacture any products, it seems only represented in a younger demographic. Could this mean that older members of society would not be able to benefit from 3 d printed projects?

In micro economy view point, although 3 D printer has benefits to individual and manufacturing consumers to reduce that their shopping or manufacturing expenditure, more design choice, raising worker individual skill and work performance. However, in macro economy view point, it also bring disadvantages to society. For example, if some members of society could not work move quickly, as a result than others, then what might be the impact upon their employability , e.g. causing unemployment of the 3D printer skillful learners who can not upgrade their working skill. Then, their employers will choose to dismiss these low skillful level 3 D printing learning skillful workers. Consequently, it will cause these member group of worker unemployment in the future society in possible. In conclusion, employers can not neglect how to train workers to learn how to apply 3 D printing skills to copy to manufacture any products.

● Massive open online course education

Will online education change traditional education? Basically, the students who choose to study from online channel, who must need have personal computers at home or school and often use internet from online platforms. In contrast to traditional methods of teaching with much small class size because every student can learn from online course at home. It means one teacher can choose to teach only one student from online channel. So, the teacher can stay at home or school as well as the student can stay at home , both of them can teach and learn from online teaching platform at the same time.

Whether the primary school, high school and university students who can accept to choose their learning habit to learn from this kind of online learning method more easily. In fact, online education will resultant impact on any teaching competitiveness. Due to , it is attempted to develop one kind of new technological education method to replace the traditional classroom by face -to-face teaching method between teacher and students contact.

However, it is not all course are suitable to adopt online teaching method and some courses re pointedly directed towards areas of interest that help education providers to also sell other online course products what other simply promote passive learning. For example, music, art, history, math, commerce courses which can be taught by teacher from online channel more easily. Because they do not need students to go to laboratory to do any experiments. Otherwise, engineering, food science, space science, medicine , doctor courses which need students go to laboratory to do experiments often. Thus, they are not suitable to be taught by teacher from online channel. Classroom teaching is more suitable to them.

Although, online teaching is low cost , due to that schools do not need many classrooms, even employ many teachers. So, they only buy computers and provide online education and less teachers are employed to teach whose students. So, it brings this question: Simply coursing cost barriers of success to education would not necessarily result in automatic take-up by young student consumers. May also need to think about best to education market, particularly to disadvantaged groups , such as older generations with lower computer and internet skills.

Who would be the winners and losers of an education market based upon such stronger principles of knowledge sharing and how can the institutions employing the use of such online or classroom or distance learning education methods be appropriately supported to maintain the high quality of further education? It seems to persuade students to choose online learning, the only method is that to let students feel online education can provide higher teaching quality level to compare traditional classroom learning method.

Other potential impacts of education market method relates more to education going online and a shift away from the more traditional forms of campus-based teaching in highest education . Would improving access to online education have the effect of increasing online students number. Due to who accept to choose online learning from traditional classroom learning habits . Thus, this is one learning habit change challenge for the traditional classroom learning students to adopt the online learning habit change.

In conclusion, for online education providers who need to consider how to change traditional classroom learning and teaching habit to adapt new online learning and teaching habit, as well as how to provide online teaching quality is higher level to compare to traditional teaching quality if who want their online education service businesses are successful.

- Future computer innovative and sustainable food source market

Future human considers health , so whose demand will high for quality of foods, farming of fish, typically freshwater with the cultivation of plants. It is simple future food source needs high health quality to provide to human to eat. If the food manufacture can have method to innovate any food quality to be more health to reduce poor health risk to influence human to eat. Thus, the food manufacturing process will be one important factor to attract consumers to choose to buy the food manufacturer's food supply. So, health food source market must attract many consumers to choose to buy to eat.

Computer technology can bring health foods supply method. Aquaponic system will be one health food manufacturing method. Aquaponic systems combine the farming of fish, typically freshwater, with the cultivation of plants. This takes place within a closed -loop aquaculture system, whereby fish are fed nutrients and their excrements one need as fertilizer directly into the water in which they are being loop. The water then feeds plants which use it for growth and filter the water , so it is suitable for re-use with the fish in the system. Such a system can be said to be closed-loop and hence a significant emphasis is placed upon the environmental and economic sustainability characteristics of acquaponic systems are only small-scale and therefore incur high costs of production relative to current methods of large-scale-farming.

However, in the future, due to human ought consider health, so who we need any food have good health quality to avoid any illness, e.g. cancer, even death causing risk from bad health foods source. In conclusion, food manufacturers need to consider any new food manufacturing methods to achieve how to manufacture foods to keep fresh and health level if they hope their food products can be attractive to consumers to choose to buy to eat.

Hence, future any new technological invention to manufacture health food will be one important factor to influence global food industry development. Also, it implies any food manufacturers need to consider how to manufacture any health foods in whose food manufacturing process. In conclusion, future foods and agriculture development will be trend to agriculture health productivity, avoidance from pests and diseases influence to food manufacturing process, avoidance food supply inequality and insecurity, more nutrition and health, changing food source manufacturing process system, reducing food losses and waste during food manufacturing process, making food systems more efficient, building resilience to protracted arises, disasters and conflicts, preventing transboundary and emerging agriculture and food system threats.

Future computer industry related service business strategy trends

- Government (public) and private partnership property development strategy

In future some business, public and private partnership method is more suitable to compare the private entrepreneur sole operation. For example, property development, construction industry example, building and rebuilding cities and new communities is a complex challenge, it requires public and private interests and resources. However, the traditional process of urban and suburban can be developed between the local government and private property developer, which will win distinctly different benefits if they decide to cooperate together.

The need to rebuild and revitalize older portions of urban areas , the public need to monetize underused assets have dramatically changes. In fact, private sole property developer's disadvantages is that it has no longer can private capital be relied on to pay the high price of assembling and preparing appropriate sites for redevelopment. Also, it has no longer can local governments bear the full burden of paying the costs of public infrastructure and facilities. If public housing department and private property developer can cooperate to achieve shared goals and objectives, this process can require applying far more effort and skill to weighing, and then balancing, public and private interests and minimizing conflicts.

For another public and private partnership example, such as health care providers and education institutions, non profit associations, such as community based organizations and business improvement district organization , these organizations are very suitable to choose to cooperate with government (public organization) to do their businesses together in the future global business environment trend.

However, the property development industry will have more benefits and needs to choose public and private partnership to compare these above industry. The main reason is that this industry will much capital to invest to any building business and it is long term tangible fixed property development business. Thus, the public and private property development partnership can implement a range of pursuits from projects to long term-plans for land use and economic growth. Partnerships have completed real estate projects, such as mixed-use developments, urban renewal through land and property assembly, public facilities, such as convention centers and airports and public services , such as affordable and military housing.

However, each public and private property development partnership is the best to share common stages with each development process as below:

In the first stage, conceptualization and initiation, stakeholders' opinions of the vision and surveyed and partners are selected through a competitive process.

In the second phase, entities document the partnership and begin to define project elements, roles and responsibilities, risks and rewards and the decision and implementation process.

In the third phase, the partnership attempts to obtain support from all stakeholders, including civil groups, local government (through entitlement), and project team members.

Finally, in the fourth phase, the partnership begins construction, leasing and occupancy and property and asset management.

However, the process is repetitions and can continue beyond the final phase when partners manage properties or initiate new projects.

For US one successful public and private property development partnership example, the contributing major benefits to the citizens of Washington, D.C. The James Foyster School Henry Adams

House, a public elementary school and 211 unit residential apartment complex was constructed as a result of a partnership among the District Of Columbia Public Schools.

● Online tourism service partnership

Another a major public and private partnership is tourism industry. Will public and private partnership to tourism be better than sole travel agent business operation? I believe it is better to any travel agent to choose public and private partnership strategy, the reasons include as below:

● Public tourism partnership goal, to provide the countries' different tourism destinations and tourism features to consider any country tourism information to assist travelers in understanding the travel problem, alternatives, opportunities and/or solutions to adapt every traveler individual travelling need.

● To obtain public travelling feedback on analysis, alternatives and/or travelling decisions, to work directly with the public throughout the travel public promotion process to ensure that public concerns and aspirations are consistent understood and considered, to partner with the public in each aspect of any tourism tickets comparison, tourism destinations, tourism entertainment, and transportation of the decision information , including the different tourism destinations development of alternatives and the identification of the preferred solution to place final decision -makings in the hands of the public.

● Every travel agent and public organization will keep every traveler's informed, listen and knowledge concerns and provide feedback on how public input influenced every tourism decision to every individual traveler considerately.

● Tourism techniques will consider fact sheet, web sites, open houses, public comment, focus tourism groups, surveys, public meetings, workshops, deliberate polling.

In conclusion, public and private partnership will be future trend to develop because capital can be shared, reduces sole business operation risks, promotes business information efficiently and easily when public organization can participate to assist these private business organization to cooperate to develop their businesses together.

- Higher education marketing, enrollment, branding and recruitment strategy

Future the most important tools for social and online education marketing will be an effective university website promotion tool to build ultimate brand for any university organization. Websites often feature elements and highlight content, including navigation, bars, engaging visuals, such as slideshows, and prominent " call to action" buttons that encourage students to apply. For example, radio ads., asking current students or for applicant referrals and online college fairs were deemed least effective, when the most effective methods of outreach open houses and campuses visit days for high school students.

Online education courses will be popular, due to adaptive learning technology has also enjoyed. So, successful branding can help increasing enrollment, expanding fundraising capabilities and other outcomes. Today, effective strategy planning and brand management require more than traditional advertising. Education institutions present and manage brand message, experience and environment achieve a competitive advantage in recruiting, building royalty among their students, parents , staff , faculty and donors.

In conclusion, how to do effective website advertising to promote university courses, website enrollment method? I shall recommend these methods as below:

Firstly, design responsive website, education institutions are placing more emphasis on responsive web design to create intuitive and easy to navigate websites that can be viewed on multiple, devices and platform.

Secondly, university administrators want their education institutions to receive a spot in search engine result particularly Google website. Especially for education institutions that offer niche programs , it is increasingly important to ensure that search

results, including the programs at the top.
Thirdly, how to use of web analytics, colleges and universities are relying on data-driven analytic to determine who, whom and where they are reaching their audiences. The use of analytics software is increasing as the higher education web ecosystem is becoming complex, e.g. domains, subdomains etc.
Fourthly, getting a better handle of this data is a new area of concentration for colleges and universities strategic social media, when recent polls indicate nearly every education institutes of higher education use some form of social media, e.g. face book or twitter account, these trends are explored.
Fifthly, the rise of mobile development and connected decides to colleges and universities for a greater amount of course content of mobile versions of websites to promote to every student to know from whose every mobile, CRM systems are heavily on content management and customer relation systems for admission for prospective students service in the future mobile promotion technology.

Bibliography

Durmaz, Yaleup and Jablonski, Sabastian, (2012): Integrated Approach To Factors Affecting Consumers Purchase Behavior In Poland And An Empirical Study. Global Journal of management and business research (GJMBR), volume 12 issue 15.
Ganesh, J., Arnold, M. and reynolds, K.E. (2000) ." Understanding The Customer Base Of Service Provides: An Examination Of The Differences Between Switchers And Stayers" , Journal of marketing, 64 (3), 65-88.
Journal of business and social science (IJBSS). volume 2, no 5, p: 105110, radford USA. http://www.ijbssnet.com /journals/ vol._2_no._5 1 special_issue_March_2011J/13,pdf
Lamb, C.W. Hair, J. F. and Mc Daniel, C. (2011): " MKTD student edition". South Western , Mason.
Priest, J., Carter, S. And Stat , D. (2013) : Consumer Behavior, Edinburgh Business School Press, United Kingdom.

Further resources.
Reed Electronic Research, Yearbook Of World Electronic Data (2003)
Taiwan Minstry Of Economic Affairs (2003)

CHAPTER TWO

Robotics technological innovation to raise computer manufacture efficiency

How robotic factor influences the computer product manufacture number

System may be physical , like the solar system or an ecological system or which may be simply behavioral, like an organization. For example, a national economy may be a system, markets are systems, firms and factories are systems. Even, families and individuals are economic systems. The economy of the largest systems, national economy, may be called macroeconomy, which deals in terms of national aggregates for output, income, productivity. The economics of small systems, which are their parts or subsystems may be called microeconomics.

A system transforms inputs into outputs. An economic system is such a process. For example, factories are as systems take in raw materials, services etc. and change them into products for sale, i.e. output and consume them, thereby transforming them into rubbish, incidential is bad output. Also, countries consume their actural resources to enhance their standard of living and change them into waste products. If the system in question is national economy, some of the subsystems are might consider to be: the government, the firms, the consumers, the natural resources which it has at its disposal. Each subsystem is itself composed of subsystem of a lower order, such as a firm and each of these can be decomposed into further subsystems, depending on the purpose of the analysis. " All subsystems" interact need have individual characteistics, i.e. they are synergistic if they expected to raise producivity or efficiency or effectively. So, it needs high technological assistance to raise whose ability in economic view.

However, an economic system must continually adapt and restructure to meet the challenges of a changing economic environment if it is to prosper. For example, a firm must respond to its environment in the form of it customers‘ needs threats from its competitors, government regulations etc. Nowadays, technological innovation process and the nature of social economic and social changes which is occurring as the same time. So, organizations need to have strategic management to raise technological innovation to achieve raising productivity and efficiency aim.

How does technological innovation occur in computer manufacture process?

What is economic process? It consists of the production and consumption of products and services by human. It is a process devised by human for own benefit pupose only. In the past, human lack advanced technological invention, e.g. family society required a much greater degree of organizational skill than hunting and gathering, it seems farming society does not need to achieve efficiency or productivity aim, because it is not industralized manufacturing society. Nowadays, the investment of resourcs is required for manufacturing processes for factories. The manufacturing stage thus needs machines, but it extends the economic process into the processing of manufacturing things, such as food. So, the knowledge and skills to do this are much more specialized again than farmer's or hunter's. So, technological innovation is needed to raise efficient productivity in factories, e.g. the increasing skills of manufacturing and the use of more intensive energy resources, such as coal and oil, gas, even solar energy either resources are from the sun or resources are from earth, e.g. fuels , heat, light, sound utilitiesm liquids , gases,solids. So, technological innovation is important to influence our economic development in our societies.

Economists usually classify what who call future of production into land, labor and capital. Why technological innovation is one another factor of production. For example, the economic process indicates that the first step is resources from the earth, e.g. solar energy supplies to earth to satisfy human needs. In the economic process, it needs these both supplies, driving force of transformation energy supply and captalyst , such as skills, knowledge, organization, creativity, creative participation in consumptions supply. Then, manufacturers shall change these both supplies to production and distribution of ordered materials and utilities in the economic process. Finally, it will provide to human consumption and human spent resources returned to earth in the final step. Another example of the elements of the economic process: the input is driving force of transformation stage of energy sources, e.g. sunlight firewood, oil and gas, coal , nuclear and household and industrial waste. Next is the economic process stage: facilitators, it includes tangible facilitator includes skills, knowledge, organization, creativity, e.g. language, science, technology, industry, machine, politics, law and order, defence, strategic plan, information systems, administration, tangible facilitator includes incentive system, e.g. money, banking, insurance, shares, private or public organizations, markets, land area. Finally, is the product of innovation stage, it includes utilities , such as electricity , heat, light, sound, motive power as well as ordered materials (products) , such as bread, meat, mine, shoes, clothes, houses, television, roads (public goods) etc.

How robotic innovation information factor influences computer manufacture eefficiency

What is the role of information? Any markets requires product or service suppliers rationally act on the basic such information. But what who can't know in advance is how all the other participants are going to behave. The market clearing price would already be known. There would in fact be agreed prices and which everything could be exchanged, and there would be no market system at all. And so who come to market to settle the price/quantity relationship. The theory is that which will arrive at a single price and quantity which reflect supply and demand. However, the number of interactions or pieces of information to be transmitted doubles with every new participants. However, the requirement for information is not limited to the particular market in question. A compromise between the number of people needed to make more nearly " perfect" in the economic sense, and the quantity of information needed to allow it to arrive at a unique price/quantity relationship. The concept of degrees of freedom is widely used in different technological forms, e.g. engineering industry, the equipment is used by manufacturers to make pencils will be worn out to some extent in the process, and this forms an energy path straight to earth from the market in which the equipment was bought. Similarly wear and tear on the equipment used to make the intermediates and the raw materials will also form direct paths to earth from the markets in which were bought. It seems technological innovation factor of production can bring the pencil stationery product innovation when the new pencil stationey product is produced the more excellent quality by the new machines innovation.

In an economic system which is working " perfectly" according to the definitations, output is therefore a function of available energy and the technological skills to apply it to conversion of inputs into materials and utilities . In a market economy, given the availability of inputs of energy and materials, and the necessary information, the only factor which can bring this about in the long term is a change in the energy efficiency of its conversion process, i.e. the energy consumed unit of output of the same total production. This depends in the application of skills and design, that is technology factor of production.

Why information can influence product sale ability. For example, the commodity is technologically complex like a computer, an aircraft or even a refrigetator. One is buying not just the piece of equipment, but also its specification because few people would understand the parts of the machine, let alone be able to judge their quality. Furthermore, one is also buying the future performance of the machine in operationm , its fuel consumptionm reliability, service costs, length of life, resistance to obsolescence etc. Probably the only guarantee that any information obtained on these points is valid is the reputation of the manufacturer. Purchasers estimate chose chances of surviving the guarante period. Brand names are a way of simplisfying information flows. Such problems of defining the commodity and so handling the information necessary to arrive at a stable price, are magnified when counterfeit products, such as are flooding on to the market at present, find their way into markets for genuine products. Buyers will be unable to distinguish unless who are experts and sometimes that may need chemical analysis or destructive testing. This is a recent phenomenon to buy technological products.

The robotic manufacture technological innovation benefits to computer manufacture factory environment

For the division of labor benefits. This is a complex process into stages in which a worker can specialize, thus allowing who to perform that particular task more efficiently, i.e. at lower cost per unit of effective output than if who had to undertake the whole process. Such an improvement in efficiency results from the more effective learning, greater development of skills and more intensive application over a period of time which becomes possible when a task is easily within the capacity of one person.

It is easily confused with advances in technology, capital investment or scale of operation. Division of complex process into stages may subsequently allow the development of specialised technologies for the individual stages, and this may result in specialised equipment, and hence capital investment . Similiarly, if the process is carried out with less labor and/or lower raw material costs for each unit of output, those concerned may in principle decide either the produce more . Output or the produce the same output with less input. It seems technological innovation can bring low cost benefits. In fact, new technology imposes a diseconomy on the old, eg. functions using old technology are at a cost disadvantage and must adopt or eventually disappear under free competition. So, new technology is the source of growth and adoptation in economy. The solutions to a diseconomy of scape lies in a change of scope, for example, in this case different establishments operating at different times, and perhaps with different prices. If capital investment are differentiated be improved to give longer life and better use, which in effect reduces their cost in use. For example, continuing advantages in technology allow processes to be designed in such a way that which deliver the same output with ever decreasing inputs of materials, labor or energy. Thus waste is minimised by planning and the conservation of process energy, and maintenance is reduced by change of design or the use of new materials. It may often worth spending more on equipment initially to reduce those time dependent costs. This sort of efficiency is the most obvious effect of scope rather than scale.

Deterioration and obsolescence means wear and tear are the changes which occur in artefacts as which are used , i.e. deterioration , or changes in quality or scope with time. These are not simply time effects because which depend both on the original design and on the conditions of use, such as maintenance skills and even simple care and attention. Obsolescence is difference to depreciation, it relates to the battle in the market place . The networks of markets brings products and therefore all conversion processes into competition for the same revenues. Old products will be not popular because which become harder to sell. Obsolescence, therefore depends not only on time, but also on competition, in the same time of business. It seems technological innovation can avoid obsolescence occurrence to old products to raise which competitive ability to the same markets. However, there was hardly an element in the competitive cost structures of conversion processes which was not disturbed in a way which differentiated country form country, industry from industry and firm from firm, such as technological innovation to any old products, which production of factor cost structures is the same basically.

The relationship between the production of factor and technological innovation in computer manufacture factory environment

Why does computer manufacture factory need to use robotic manufacture tools to replace human workers in computer manufacture factory environment ?The term "innovation" is used to describe the deliberate process by which a new product or process comes to be sold in the market. Technology innovation can be applied to conversion processes, which requires the use of energy, or their products, which have an economic energy content. It is therefore a function of all the forces which shape markets: manufacturing, processing, technology, buying, selling, information, prices costs etc. So an innovating organization may be a whole company or it may be an individual. Other forms of innovation (production of factor) relate to the sale of services within what defines as the facilitiation system. That sort of exchange is not specifically considered to be one production of factor, because it involves different adoptation processes and response times, and doesn’t of itself add to the quantity of products or utilities sold.

However, invention can not be defined to one production of factor and it is to be distinguished to innovation. We can describe invention is as the process of discovering something completely new, i.e. a new fact or relationship. It is an important scientific advance. Invention enlarges the scope of man's awareness, but it doesn't necessarily have direct economic value in itself. If it is sold, it is the sale of an idea, an exchange of a little creativity for an incentive within the facilities system. It isn't marketed as a new product of a conversion process. No energy of conversion is involved. The great majority of inventions do not enter into the economic process and which do not become innovations until that happens.

What is the process of robotic technological innovation in the computer manufacture factory environment ?

If the change of scope results in a new process for making a product or utility which is already being sold, this can't be differentiated from the existing product or utility in the market concerned. To be successful the new process must make it at lower unit cost than existing process. The result then is that either the price of the product fulls and processes to improve are imposed to competition or more net revenue is accumulated. So the aims of the factors of technological innovation production include: The introduction of a process for making at a lower unit cost a non-differentiated product which is sold into a commodity market, and the development and sale of a differentiated product which will draw buyers away from other markets, or draw money into the market which would not otherwise have been spent.

The nature of technological innovation how causes factor of production. The process of technological innovation is the arrangement of materials at the elementary, say atomic or molecular level, or of components or the design of new machines, or of the relative positions of components, for example, the location of nodes in networks. There are the three levels at which the scope of the economic process may be changed. However, technological innovation can't seem without some change in the way materials ae ordered. It follows that all technological innovation flows initially from some change in a conversion process. Thus technological in the result of investment in conversion processes, where investment is defined as laying down fixed assets and so it requires a change in the use of energy consumed during conversion to make useful products. The flexible manufacturing system themselves are examples of the third level of innovation, the spatial arrangement of components and hence the link between them. Patterns of communication have changed and are continue to change as a result of new technoloby in the use of energy and the convergence of computer, data maipulation and telecommunication. Flexible manfacturing systems manufacture components in rather than having them made by supplies industries and transported to an assembly plant in batches. The new arrangements reduce both the time of reponse to market changes and all the skills of components which are needed to give flexibility of response in conventional systems , i.e. they give economy of scope.

How to raise efficient short manufacture response times in computer manufacture factory technological innovation manufacture environment?

In the terminology which have developed above, the behavioral effects may be considered as adjustment of the scope of the sellers and buyers organizations as the process of acceptance of the innovation in the market proceed. Costs and risks in technological innovation, innovation requires the commitment of resources over a long period, and it is therefore subject to the same kind of risks as any investment in conversion processes. The most obvious risk is that the technological difficulties are in the initial concept, with the result that no returns will be earned and the resources sunk in the investment may have been wasted. There is a set of market-related reasons why technological success may not result in an innovation. By the time, the new process or product is ready for the market, the demand for it may have receded or may never have materialised.

This may be the result of fulfiment of the potential users' needs by another technology, i.e. the innovation may be technologically obsolete before it may be because of a change of fashion or styles of living.

Two conclusions may be drawn, firstly, the product manufacturer has a good foresight and understanding is needed when undertaking projects which consume large amount of capital, or it may result in gross waste, because the future is always uncertain, however, the analysis, secondly, there is a limit to the rate of constructive innovation in an economic system, the ratio at which the system can accumulate. Hence, some product manufacturer will feel the technological innovation can be a good production of factor , such as a cost advantage is termed a competitive advantages. It is a broader term than the comparative advantages of traditional economy because of does not depend on a favorable climate or an abundance of natural resource. It is developed and maintained entirely by the skills of the people in the firms which are involved.

Technology is like on the economic process, because once knowledge about transforming inputs into outputs has been obtained, and especially after it has been implemented, it doesn't disappear. Technological innovation moves the whole process. Thus, economy of scope confer permanent advantages on those who have them. Economy of scope is to be obtained from all the elements of the economic process which change with time and these are suspectible to improvement, whether as separate elements. They involve people, and their capacity to learn and improve, and material in all their different forms.

Why does robotic technological innovation will be one factor of production to computer technological manufacture factory industry.

Innovation is the process by which new products‘ processes methods or services are created. Innovation offers added value for and users by providing better and/or cheaper functionality than previous options. Innovation combines changes in technology, business models, organization etc. The basic idea may be a new technical solutions, a new business model or a change in organization. In a competitive economy, no business can survive long term without updating its products and services or the ways in which are produced or delivered. Innovation policy must promote renewal across all business sectors and not just focus on high technological industries.

Since most innovations are complex and each subsystem has its own limitation , an important part of the innovation process is finding the right balance between conflicting demands. In most cases, there are several possible ways of providing a new function to users, or possible applications of a new technology. Which combination of features the market will prefer can't be predicted with any certainty. Whether the origin was a market opportunity on a new technological capability to one part of the production of factor to the product.

Innovation integrates knowledge from a number of different fields: technology, marketing, design, economic etc. In the production of factor view, it is hard to collect all the necessary competences in a single organization. Because technological products need to be updatd to keep competition in market. Thus, innovation has become a process of constant with suppliers and competitors, with consultants and with academic researchers. In the production of factor view, the capacity to innovate depends on how well different parts of this system are adapted to each other and how well they work together.

Today, the relationship between science and innovation is more complex and interdependent. Science-based technologies, such as microelectronics or biotechnology could not have been developed without scientific understanding, but modern science is equally dependent on advanced technology. Economists tend to prefer technology performance standards, but these risk favouring marginal improvements to existing technologies when discouraging more radical, long term solution. Also, economists tend to think of innovation as a production processes. A more production describes innovations as an experimental learning proces in which organizations and individuals build new competence. This term "research-based competence" is rather than " science-based knowledge or "scientific information".

I shall argue that economists' active process is a better way of think about the relationship between industry and academic research. Whether can the production of factor of technological innovation make use of the tools and results of research in addressing real world problem to manufacture any technological products? This main concern at the time was whether research and innovation were essentially different activities which should be supported in different ways or whether it was important to deal with both aspects together since which were interdependent. However, innovation is a process of searching, experimenting and learning. Consumers can learn about how new products, processes and services are created, how firms build competence for this and what information sources which use. So, I feel technological innovation ought be one part of production process or production of factor to some manufacturers. Such as, searching is needed for better ways of doing worth which things. Experimenting is needed because consumers can't seen in advance the best way of accomplishing a desired outcome or indeed what users really want or need. Learning is needed because actors involved in an innovation process will learn from it. The kind of learning which changes consumers' ability to solve future challenges and opportunities. However, economists often think of innovation is as a production prcocess, where knowledge transformed into a new product. We measure research and development investment, relating these to outcomes in the form of patents, new products and productivity or economic growth. Innovations are not just new technological products or processes, it also mentions organizational innovations, new distribution channels, new business models etc. In fact, it is often misleading to think about technical or organizational innovation as separate processes. Most innovations combine changes in technology, business models organization etc. in production process.

What kinds of product can belong to high technological manufacturing. For example, the world's most advanced steel plants and paper mills can never be classified as high technology because of their complementary need for high levels of investment in fixed capital, and aerospace manufacture is classified as medium technology. The standard definition of high technology measures research and development intensity not the generation or use of advanced technology as such. A far better measure is the proportion of scientists, engineers and highly qualified technicians in the labor force. For computer industry example, innovations in the field of rabotic manufacturing, nanotechnologies and human genetics research all have been enabled by low cost computational and control capabilities supplied by computers and software. Reducing the cost of software important objectives of the U.S. software industry. However, the complexity of the software industry to support the U.S. is computerized economy is increasing at an alarming rate. Software nonperformance and failure are expensive. In actuality many factors contribute to the quality issues facing the software industry. These include marketing strategies, limited liability by software vendors, and decreasing returns to testing.

At the core of these issues is the difficulty in defining and measuring software reliability, usability, efficiency, maintenability and portability. Information problems are further complicated by the fact that even with substantial testing, software developers don't truly know how their products with perform until who encounter real scenarios. The similiar industries with need have technological innovation in the productive process (production of factor), such as automotive and aerospace equipment manufacturers and related electronic communications equipment manufacturers. Quality is defined as attribute factor to different kinds of software product. Defining the attributes of software quality and determining the metrics to access the relative value of each attribute are not formalized processes. Because users place different values on each attribute depending on the product's use, it is important that quality attributes be observable to consumers. The technological innovation is one production of factor to software industry. Due to software attributes have those accurateness, interoperability, security, reliability (maturity, recoverability); usability (understandability, learnability, operability); efficiency (time behavior, resource behavior); maintainability (analyzability, changeability, stability, testability); portability (abaptability, installability, replaceability). It seems that due to software attribute have these characteristics, so it causes technological innovation is one production of factor to software industry.

Nowadays, human needs have been increasing, external factor can influence some industries cause technological innovation is one production of factor need. Together, these tends are going to reshape now human live and work, reorganize our social, economic and political institutions and redistribute power and reward in society. In the longer term, as machine learning and computer power intelligence technological innovation needs from consciousness, as machine learning and computer from consciousness, as improving health technologies allow for biological enhancements and species divergence, and as the final frontier is also needed by space travel, technological and social transformation will increasingly change what is means to be human. However, human have to better understand how our world is changing and by what forces those changes are driven . So, because human have high living quality needs, so it causes many new products have technological innovation to manufacture new product or to raise high quality need to satisfy our daily life. It will cause of factor to some products.

The technological innovation factor can influence the economic of the pork meat production in agricultural industry. For example, the economy of the pork meat production on a farm has been carried out with the help of the method of production functions (factor-product and factor-factor). The influence of the weight of an animal on the daily growth tells us that the growth is increased with the increse of the entry weight to 19kg and with the exit weight of the fattened animal of 100 kg. So, the relationship between the daily growth and the feed costs by a feeding day shows us the tendency of than increase of a daily growth with the increase of the feed costs, e.g. with the increase of labor inputs to 2.6 hours/ 100 kg of the live weight and the increased profit to 29 monetary units. Labor productivity grows with the increase of the capacity usage to 87% and then it decrease. The economy of agricultural production considerably depends on the development of cattle-breeding as a natural capacity of transforming plant products into high quality cattle products. Cattle-raising production influences the food quality, the development of food production industry, the output of high quality and healthy safe product and the development of agricultural economy. So, it seems technological innovation can be a production of factor to influence farm agricultural industry to assist farmers to apply high, e.g. agricultural technology (skills) produces high quality and tastic of farming met to satisfy consumers' diet needs.

Growth of total factor productivity (TFP) can provide society with an opportunity to increase the welfare of people. In particular, in the simplest framework, change in labor productivity factor depends on change (TFP) and capital deepening. How to change TFP? I shall suppose the technological innovation method is a factor to reduce labor cost, but it can raise labor productivity and products or goods of quality to satisfy consumers‘ needs in competitive market. Economists often define the knowledge economy as production and services based on knowledge-intensive activities tht contribute to an accelerated pace of technical and scientific technology, as well as rapid absolescence. Knowledge is now recognized as the driver of productivity and economic growth, leading to a new focus on the role of information, technology and learning in economic performance. In the knowledge-based economy, innovation is driven by the interaction of producers and users in the exchange of both codified and tacit knowledge: This interactive model has replaced the traditional linear model of innovation. The knowledge-intensive and high technology, economy tends to be the most dynamic in terms of output and employment growth. Changes in technology and particularly the advent of information technologies are making educated and skilled labor more valuable, and unskilled labor less. So, the technological innovation production of factor will bring skilled labor needs, more and unskilled labor needs less.

Although, it can maximize the benefits of technology for productivity, but it can raise unemployment number of non-skillful labor, because the high technological product firms will choose to dismiss the non-skillful labor and will employ skillful labor when innovation which decide to apply technological innovation method to produce whose products. For example, output and employment are expanding fastest in high technology industries, such as computers, electronic and aerospace. Also, knowledge-intensive service sectors, such as online education, communication and information(long distance call) are growing even faster, such as internet shopping technological business can be production of factor to let universities can teach students from internet, such as distance learning. Internet can be used to adventise and sell products from businessman individual website more easily. Also, mobile can use internet to do same benefits, such as laptop or desktop kinds of high technological computer products. It seems technological benefits can attract consumer individual consumption more easily. So, skillful biased technical change is a shift in the production technology that favors skilled over unskilled labor by increasing its relative productivity and therefore, its relative demand. In fact, skill-biased technical change is a shift in the production technology (factor of production that favors skilled, e.g. more relative productivity) and therefore, its relative demand.

How can external and internal factors affect the desktop and laptop product in computer manufacture process innovation?

In fact, the competition advantages of a computer software or laptop or desktop company strongly depends on its possibility to benefit from robotic manufacture innovational activities. Understanding the factors how which affect product and process innovation and their effort is necessary to be proved why innovational activities can be the one part production of factors to some new products. It has close relationship between product and business processes innovation and industry maturity and customer needs (demand) technological opportunities and investment attractiveness and company size and export orientation. These external and internal factors can influence innovational activities to some new products.

Nowadays, fast technology development, combined with the globalization and fast changes in with the globalization and fast changes in customer demand, implies that a competitive advantage of a company. So, companies will spans great effort in beating the competition innovations have a vital influence on economic development of a country. On the macro level, innovations have a vital influence on economic development that innovations are more and more present both a developed and developing countries that wish to grow developing countries that wish to grow fast and become developed. If we simply categorize companies all innovative or non-innovative. Among different innovation's categorizations is developed by researchers, the most important are: classification according to the type of innovation to degree of innovativity, innovations can be classified as incremental, semi-radical and radical innovations (Davila et al 2006), who indicates that radical innovations potentially offer huge profits and competitive advantage, but demand considerably high risk level, much company effort need and resource engagement. Otherwise, incremental innovations have more modest returns, but demand lower risk level, level of efforts and resources and are generally more successful. Finally, semi-radical innovations are somewhere between the two of them.

According to (Christensen 2003) explained to an innovations can be sustaining and disruptive. Sustaining innovations can be placed in the whole range from incremental to radical and discuptive are either semi-radical or radical. Sustaining innovations are those that improve existing products or process, disregarding the degree of improvement. Disruptive innovations create a huge growth offering a new of performances which has even it is inferior from the start comparing to existing technologies' performances a potential to become superior. Companies are advised to accept what is the best for their situation and design innovational processes, develop aptitudes, allocate resources and form partnerships in compliance to that decision.

In fact, many external and internal factors can affect companies chose product innovations, because process, innovations or their combination, e.g. factors include industry maturity, customer needs and expectations , technological opportunities, investment attractiveness, intensity of cmpetition, company size, origin of ownership and export orientation. In the industry maturity stage, as a market matures and customer needs become defined in a better way, companies transfer the focus of their competition to expenses and economy of range investing more in business processes in order to make them more effective and more efficient. Customer needs and expectations are essential for process innovations that improve process effectiveness. Orientation to customers and their satisfaction are well-known concept in the field of a total quality management.

The point of view that market demand presents the main determine the rate and activities of an invention because each rational company that tends to make profit is responsive to economic stimuli . According to Schmookler (1962) demand growth is prior to the growth in innovative activites, i.e. market requests guarantee stimuli for companies to innovate and take up new technologies. This concept is popularly called " market pull" in a sense that a market pulls innovations.

What does computer production innovation process mean in knowledge manufacture economy ?

I shall give evidences to explain why technological innovation can be one kind of production factor to some technological product manufacture industry nowadays. Nowadays, we are entering the knowledge based economy stage. Knowledge is now recognized as the driver of productivity and economic growth, leading to new focus or the role of information technology and learning in economic performance. The knowledge based economy and its relationship is as traditional economics, as reflected in “ new growth theory”. Because every technological product manufacturer needs workers to acquire a range of skills and to continuously adapt these skills underlines the “ learning economy”. The importance of knowledge and technology diffusion requires better understanding of knowledge networks and “ national innovation systems”.

Firstly, knowledge-based economies which are directly based on the production, distribution and use of knowledge and information. The is reflected in the trend in growth in high technology investment, high technological industries, move highly-skilled labor and associated productivity gains. Also required is tacit knowledge including the skills to use and adapt codified knowledge-based economy, innovation is driven by the interaction of producers and users in the exchange of both codified and tacit knowledge.

Employment in the knowledge-based economy is characterized by increasing demand for more highly skilled workers. The knowledge-intensive and high-technology tend to be the most dynamic in terms of output and employment growth. The science system, essentially public research laboratories and institutes of highest education, carries out key functions in the knowledge-based economy, including knowledge production, innovative technology. So, the traditional functions of producing new knowledge through basic research and educating new generations of scientists and engineers with its newer role of collaborating with industry in the transfer of knowledge and technology. For example, our societies tend to research institutes and academic increasingly have industrial partners for financial as well as innovative purposes, but most combines this with their essential role in more generic research and education.

In general, our understanding of what is happening in the knowledge-based economy is constrained by the extent and quality of the available knowledge-rated indicators. So, available knowledge-rated indicated. So, development of indicators of the knowledge-based economy must start with improvements to more traditional input indicators of research and development expenditures and research personal. Better in indicators are also needed of knowledge stocks and flows, particularly relating to the diffusion of information technologies, in both manufacturing and service sectors; social and privates rates of return to knowledge investments to the impact of innovation technology in productivity and growth.

However, knowledge is such as human being (human capital) and in innovative technology has always been central to economic development. When human is entering the 21 ST century, our output and employment are expanding tastes in high technology industries, such as computers, electronics and aerospace investment is thus being directed to high-technology products and services, particularly information and communicating technologies. Computers and related equipment are the fastest growing component of tangible investment. Equally important are more intangible investments in research and development, the training of the labor force, computer software and technical expertise. Hence, it causes employment is growing in high technology, science-based sectors ranging from computers to pharmaceuticals. Also, research and development causes manufacturing sector is losing jobs. Due to those jobs are more highly skilled and pay higher wages than those in lower technology sectors (e.g. textiles and food processing). Knowledge-based jobs in service sectors are also growing strongly. Indeed, non-production or knowledge workers those who don't engage in the output of physical products, are the employees in most demand in a wide range of activities from computer technicians, through physical therapists to marketing specialists.

Economists continue to search for the foundations of economic growth. Traditional, " production functions" focus on labor, capital , materials and energy, land; however, knowledge and technology are external influence on production. Analytical approaches are being developed. So, that knowledge can be included more directly in production functions. Investment in knowledge can raise productive capacity of the other factors of production as well as transform them into new products and processes from innovative technology.

According to the neo-classical production function, returns diminish is as more capital is added to the economy an effect which may be offset, however, by the flow of new technology. In new growth theory, knowledge can raise the returns on investment, which can contribution to the accumulation of knowledge. Technological change can also raise the relative marginal productivity of capital through education and training of the labor force, investment in research and development and the creation of new managerial structures and worth organization. In fact, incorporating knowledge into standard economic production functions is not easy task, as this factor defies some fundamental economic principles, such as that of scarcity, knowledge is intangible, but labor, capital, land, equipment etc. production of factors which can be tangible or measured. However, some kinds of knowledge can be easily reproduced and distributed at lower cost to abroad set of users, which tends to undermine private ownership.

Knowledge is a much broader concept than information, which is generally the " know-what", and "know-why" components of knowledge. There are also the types of knowledge which come closet to being market commodities or economic resources to be fitted into economic production functions.

Knowledge can divide know-why and know-how both kinds of concept. Know-why means to scientific knowledge of the principles and laws of nature. This kind of knowledge underlines technological development and product and process advances in most industries. The production and reproduction of know-why is often organized in specialized organizations, such as research-laboratories and universities. Otherwise, know-how means to skills or the capability to do something. Business judging market prospects for a new product or a personnel manager selecting and training staff have to use their know-how. The same is true for the skilled worker operating complicated machine tools. Finally, knowledge-who becomes increasingly important. Know-who involves information about who knows what and who know how to do what. It involves the make if possible to get access to experts and use their knowledge efficiently. So, knowledge economy brings those conditions to our societies. One hypothesis is that globalization and international competition have led to decrease relative demand for less-skilled workers of the phenomenon; an alterative explanation is that innovative technology change has become more strongly biased in favor of skilled workers, changes in firm behavior is as the main reason for falling real wages for low-skilled workers. Thus, innovative technology and knowledge economy has close relationship to cause knowledge workers can bring high technological products of production of factor in technological product manufacture industry.

computer production internal robotic technical skill

Secondly, it is the internal skill biased technical change influences. Skill-biased technical change is a shift in the production technology, that flavors skilled over unskilled labor by increasing its relative productivity and , therefore, its relative demand of innovative technology of production factor. The direction of technical changes i.e. whether new capital complements skilled or unskilled labor may be determined by innovators' economic incentives shaped by relative prices, the size of the market and institutions.

Economic theory views the production technology as a function describing that a collection of factor inputs can be transformed into output, and it defines technical change as a shift in the production of function. In fact, given who observed movements of the production function only concentrates on , such as land supply, labor numbers, equipment supply, capital demand factors. Therefore,To make sense of these recent developments, the concept of factor biased technical change can be another production of factor to influence the new technical products quantities change. For example, the timing of the rise in the skill premium has changed the rapid diffusion of information and communication technologies in the workplace environment in any high technological industry generally nowadays. For example, expenditures in information processing equipment and software, is as a share of U.S. private non-residential fixed investment, rose from 6% in 1960 year to 40% in 2000 year. At the heart of those dynamic change.

This is an improvement in the quality and productivity of all those equipment products, relying heavily on semiconductors like computers, software and switching equipment underlying much of communication technology. In the early adoption phase of a new technology, that those who adapt more quickly can reap some benefits. As time goes by, there will be enough makers learning how to work with the new technology to offset the wage differential. Note the difference with the hypothesis set, where the effect of capital deepening on the skill premium is permanent. Also, information technologies production of factor can reduce costs of data storage, communication, monitoring and supervision activities within the firm which causes a shift towards a new organizational design. In particular, the layers in the hierarchical structure can be reduced, so that the organization of the firm becomes "flatter". So, workers no longer perform routinized, responsible for a wide range of tasks within teams. Therefore, adaptable workers verses at multi-tasking activities benefits is a factor of production to reduce internal cost of any firms.

Due to technological innovation causes the layers in the hierarchical structure can be reduced, so that the organization of the firm becomes "flatter". How technological innovation can influence internal skill biased technical change to orgnizational structure. Development behavioral means it is through managment theory. So, high technological skillful organization will choose to apply theory x more than theory y because this technological innovation will reduce some unskillful staffs and give more effort and duties to those skillful staffs to use high technological skill to do whose jobs daily and who will feel lazy and unhappy to do extra more technological jobs. Theory x assumptions are the average human being dislike of work and work avoid if who can, most people must be controlled, directed or threatened with punishment to adequate effort to action organization objective; otherwise, theory y assumptions are people like to use physical and mental effort to work as natural as play and rest, human being dislike work, a source of satisfaction, threat of punishment are not being effort. Hence, technological innovation can cause organizations to change whose structure and skill staffs need to do more jobs. It causes employer need to give extristic and intrinsic motivations to satisfy whose skillful staffs needs to raise efficiency, e.g. giving more tangible reward, as salary, benefit, security, promotion, good contract of condition of work service, comfortable workplace environment as well as using one ability to achieve who feel apprecation, positive being treating of psychological satisfactory needs.

In technological innovation of organization structure, the management committee needs to concern whose skillful technological labor individual psychological needs. Because technological innovation is one important production of factor and it has close relationship between motivation and staff individual efficiency and productivity. As Maslow's hierarchy of needs indicates people (staffs) mean having satisfied to achieve motivation behavior, the lowest love is basic physiological, the need for food, as salary, safe working condition, then is job security, benefit. Next is friendship at work group, after is promotion, payment increasing, high status of job title. Finally is achievement in work advancement opportunitie creative task in related aspect at work motivation. Hence, after the traditional non-technological innoviation of organization changed the technological innovation of organizational structure, management needs to concern that motivation is needed to develop of behavioral through contributed to management theory. Every organiztion manageer needs to know what its team staffs whose indvidual needs, it includes extrinsic needs, e.g. salary, promotion, security as well as intrinsic needs, e.g. achievement, appreciaton. If the employees feel extrinsic needs are more than intrinsic needs, the managers can consider what extrinsic needs, the managers can consider what extrinsic needs of whose employee individual need. If the employee feels intrinsic needs are more than extrinsic needs, the manage can consider what intrinsic needs the employee individual actual need in order to motivate the skillful worker to work efficiently and raising productivity.

After changing the technological innovation of organizational structure, the management needs to concern how to plan to raise its productivity from its production of factor of technological innovation. Planning is looking ahead, control is looking back, every organization must need strategic plan, operative plan and tastic plan for every department to give aim for its mission objectives. Then it needs to achieve its any short term plans or long term plans efficiently, e.g. how to achieve to produce and to sell 5,000 computers sale objective or how to increase to achieve 20% profit or productivity objective from 10% within one year. So, after the technological innovation production of factor influences the organization needs to find reasons what how to influence it can not achieve these new objectives within one year. Then, it needs to find reasons and revises to solve challenges to control it can achieve it's planning objectives. For example, SWOT method indicates what its internal strengths and weaknesses, external threats and opportunities are. To aim achieve its planning strategic plan every year. Before the organization is not technological innovation, it can't have control is looking ahead, due to planning is looking back because organization can;t know what it's mission and objectives can't achieve to revise if it has no any strategic plan, operational plan and tactical plan for top, middle and low level to let different department managers to know what it's mission and objectives are planned to achieve before the organization has not changed the technological innovation of organizational structure in the year. Besides, after the technological innovation changed the organizational structure. The management needs to concern how to implement it's strategies effectively. The technological innovation of organization needs to change its old long term strategic plan to be new long term strategic plan in the top level, e.g. one year what is its new mission for its technologcial innovation, e.g. Apple brand of computer company needs to innovate its old style computer design to know how to adapt the young client group needs (demand) in this competitive computer technological product industry.

Finally, after innovative organizational structure, mangement needs to concern how to raise skillful labor individual productivity and efficiency, due to who need to increase more effort to do their jobs after technological innovation. I shall indicate on job training method. The advantages on limitations of different approaches to on the job training include the company needs to spend extra time and resources to train staffs or workers to work, when who are on the regular work time. Hence, it will lose staffs to do regular job duties, due who needs to learn how to do their job. So the employer needs to pay higher salary to every job trainer for long term if it needs to train many skillful labor after technological innovation. It can't ensure whether the training employees can work efficiently and know who are not the right staffs to get training. Hence, it will employ the staffs who are not right staffs to accept job training riskly if the mangement have not evaluate who have effort to be train to raise whose productivity and testing personal effort of evaluation is more important to the job trainers.

What are the technical change as exogenous or endogenous computer production of factor?

Finally, I shall indicate what the change is as exogenous or endogenous factor in the production function model to cause innovative technology to produce new technological product in computer or software manufacture industry. Although, economic theory firstly treated technology change is as a residual, the unexplained part remaining after the contribution of an increased quantity and quality of capital, labor and natural resources in output growth have been accounted for. However, the theory of economic growth reconsidered recently the nature of technological change and the concept of knowledge. Therefore, the new growth economic theory includes research and development is as a factor of influence in the macroeconomic models.

The endogenous or exogenous nature of technological change refers to its source: endogenous is internal to the national economy, being created by domestic private or public enterprise, when exogenous change is external originating from foreign sources. So, it seems research and development workforce is as new factor in the production function model. Although, technological progress, managerial improvements and innovation in general are nowadays largely regarded as key contributors to economic growth. Schumpeter (1939) defines technical progress in terms of production function, which describes the way the production output varies according to the quantity and quality of the input factors. So, the technological change represents the factor that shifts the production function.

From the theoretical viewpoint, it has difficult to separate knowledge from the other factors of the production function. The total labor factor productivity is usually estimated by output the capital and labor factors, weighted by their specific shares. Under perfect competition, the price of the production factors is equal to their marginal productivity, hence, their shares in outputs are equal to their exponents from the production function.

Otherwise, from the empirical point of view, there are difficulties of measurement, especially in the case of value added and research-development variables. So, from all available data on research and development input and outputs, research and development expenditures are most frequently used, along with the number of patents, the technological balance of payments, machinery and tools inputs etc. costs to measure of input in innovation.

Furthermore, the exponents of the new growth theory indicates modeled knowledge is as an output quality of the research and development sector and proved that contrary to the neoclassical conclusions of the diminishing-returns technology, the introduction of the human capital changes the production function into one with increasing returns. Thus, it seems total research and development expenditures are used in this model as a measure of total investments (material and intangible) in the research and development sector. However, in many studies, the research and development stock is calculated as the accumulated value of research and development expenditure after depreciation, a procedure which implies the assumption that all of the research and development expenditure certainly and that it's stock depreciates with a certain fixed rate. Since, long time-series data on R & D are rarely available, other studies assume that the growth rate of R & D expenditure to R & D stock is stable. Hence in innovation technological industry, the labor production factor can be divided into two components total employees population outside the research development sector and the number of employees in research and development. The same types of division was applied to the capital production factor.

Reference

Christensen, C.M. (2003) " the innovator's dilema", Harpercollins, New York.

Davila, T., Epstein, M. J., Shelton.R. (2006) " Making innovation work: How to manage it, measure it and profit from it". Warton school publishing, New Jersey.

Schmookler, J., (1962) " Economic sources of incentive activity, " the journal of economic history. vol. 22
, no. 1 (Mar. 1962), 1-20.

Schumpeter, J., A. (1939), business cycles: A Theoretical Historical And Statistical Analysis Of Capitalist Processes, New York: Macmillan.

CHAPTER THREE

Internet market development trend

What is Internet entertainment function

The internet is one of the most used platforms in the world today particularly because of its limitless access to information from different subjects and times in history. The internet and its uses play a very critical role in the life of each and every individual, especially the literate ones and can most be appreciated in the 21st Century.

Will future internet be main entertainment need?

I believe future the internet is used for research purposes mainly because it has unrestricted access to a vast amount of data from all parts of the world and over. Moreover, internet is also used for communication purposes through protocols such as email and many more in that it provides a platform through which information can be sent hence bridges geographical gap. For example, download and upload of files is also another significant use of the internet, where the subject is able to access different files due to the permission the internet has, as well as send information. It does not matter where the files were uploaded from.

In internet entertainment function aspect, video game players can also achieve conduction of interactive games as well as discussion groups over the internet regardless of the groups' geographical position in that all of you could b at different corners of the world. In Education and self-improvement aspect, teachers can also be done over the internet by making reference to multiple educational materials available over the internet. Electronic newspapers and magazines fall here. It is also possible to make friends and even date over the internet by provisions such as chatting and even making video calls.

Is internet one popular tool useful to future communication aspect? Internet has these different unique characteristics:

- Internet has made almost unlimited amounts of information available to everyone.
- Since many official procedures are available online, internet has dramatically reduced the processing time for them such as registration of a business, application for a passport etc.
- Critical information, such as the traffic situation on road or air etc. is easily available avoiding many harassing situations for passengers.
- Internet has made commerce very easy. People can browse the online shops virtually and make payments for shopping online.
- Learning has become easier due to the information and learning material that is available online.
- Many courses can be conducted online thus making distance learning much more feasible.
- Internet banking has made transfer of funds much easier. One doesn't have to carry around cash in large amounts.
- Because of internet the availability of jobs also goes up as online jobs with no location restriction become easier.
- Quality of work of all kinds improves since the candidate pool for any job is bigger.
- For readers, all kind of books available at one's finger tips, many of them free of cost, online.
- Internet also makes it easy for people to connect on issues close to their hearts. Parents from across the globe and discuss children's issues etc., which works as a support group.
- Entertainment has become easily available through internet media such as YouTube.
- Internet has made social contacts much easier to maintain.

- Crime can be reduced if social media is used as an awareness tool.
- Internet has also made medical issues easier to handle by sharing the reports and diagnosis of a patient through email etc.
- Pictures and videos can be easily shared over the internet.
- Video apps on the internet have made video calls not just possible but also common getting people closer.
- Paying bills etc. is also much easier due to internet making life much simpler especially for the elderly.
- A young mother can watch her toddler in a day care while she works through the CCTV connected to the internet.
- Internet makes it easier to reach out to the experts across the globe for consultations if necessary because of the internet.

The media is analyzed in two ways here as an informative aspect as well as a form of entertainment.Freedom of expression is usually questioned in the media, how 'free' is the media allowed to be? Isn't the media always controlled? What is the role of media in society, for entertainment aim, I shall explain the reasons internet will not be the suitable entertainment media aim as below:

Is everyone in society treated equally in the media, when being reported on from internet channel? It is often a belief that the media is a rather powerful tool, one that gets blamed for all the wrong that occurs in society. What we read in the papers and view on television is usually what we believe.

What is functionalism to internet entertainment aim?:

Functionalism refers to a system, a belief in function over form. Functionalism with regard to the media – refers to how the media operates as a whole 'system' in society to help create a balance in society. Society as an integrated, harmonious and cohesive whole. Different social systems function to maintain equilibrium, consensus and social order. Media as a powerful socialization instrument should contribute towards integration, harmony and cohesion through information, entertainment and education.

Functions of the internet entertainment media:

Main functions of the media are – to inform and entertain, this allows the media to contribute manifestly or latently to cultural growth for individuals and society. Though its rather a simplistic model especially when it comes to the political functions of the media

Objections (Short comings) to internet entertainment aim functionalism:

Functionalism takes for granted that agreement prevails over, and disregards conflict in society. The media will not have the same functions for all the people in society. Interpreted differently by individuals. Cultural barriers could arise when interpreting different media Functionalism does not account for social change well established democratic societies Vs societies in the process of transformation. Neglects to provide for feedback (seeing that feedback modifies both the message and the context)

If future internet can bring entertainment aim to provide information about events and conditions in society and the world, facilitate innovation, adaptation and progress for human entertainment aim, it will be worth technological tool. e.g. express the dominant culture and recognize subcultures and new cultural developments provide amusement, diversion and the means of relaxation entertainment aim, reduce social tension and provide social objectivity in issues such as war and politics and economic development.

Future internet will need to be one fun entertainment media should exist in various forms such as radio, television, and print among other forms catering for all of society. Think of DSTV as an example does a wide range of channels mean a wider range of program content? Are more groups of people catered for with the diversity of channels? To criticize political developments and decisions. Internet entertainment media policy ensures media pluralism (the existence of different media: various newspapers, radio stations, television stations, magazines, films and so on.Internet needs to provide these entertainment message, e.g. differences within the information and entertainment content of newspapers, radio and television stations ® should be balanced, offer different opinions etc. differences between different newspapers, radio and television stations. Concerns all the media, regardless of category, available in a society; the variety of choices.

Internet entertainment media should be able to publish what they see fit, the media is also allowed to publish information against the ruling power and society should interpret the messages accordingly. People are rational beings capable of distinguishing between truth and falsehood, and between good and evil. Give them all factual information and let them decide. Its the responsibility of the internet media to keep the citizens of a country duly informed of the actions of its government. Internet entertainment media needs to be basic on these assumptions as below:

The media is a source of information.

The media is a platform for expression of divergent opinions.

Free from government control.

Media should be free from external censorship.

Should be accessible to any individual or group.

Editorial attacks should not be punishable.

No coercion to publish anything.

No restrictions on the acquisition of information.

No restrictions on import and export of information across borders

The media should be free from censorship that is external from it, so that certain officials from a political party can't restrict or delete certain remarks that were made to the public because they would want to dictate what the public reads and what not.

– Publication should be free without a licence for the people reading the material. There are no restrictions like this in South Africa currently.

– If there are any "editorial attacks" on government it should not be punishable; this paves the way for free speech like the article of Boyle, giving his opinion and informing the public.

– There should be no compulsion to publish anything as this will give an unjust and skew view of what is happening in South Africa. With parties exerting their power to help their own cause.

– The "acquisition of information" should not be restricted if they are obtained through legal channels. For instance the number of South African Police Service members that were suspended because of corruption – those are available thus it can be published if the journalist wishes and to inform the public.

– There should be no restriction so that information about the country may or may not be imported or exported.

Social responsibility theory:

Internet entertainment Media should be equal and fair in its reporting of incidents and issues. It must be diverse and responsible towards society. The social responsibility to internet entertainment media may include: Reconcile the ideas of freedom and independence with responsibility towards society, media should support democratic political principles, create a form for different viewpoints and should meet certain standards.

Internet entertainment media should accept responsibility towards society. They include as below:

Set professional standards (truth, accuracy, objectivity, balance)

Avoid information that could lead to crime, violence or social disruption. Not offend ethnic or religious minorities.

Be representative of all social groups. Reflect the diversity of society.

Intervention if the media fail to meet these standards.

Media must work and be owned by the working class.

Main assumptions:

Act in the interest of, and be controlled by the working class.

Media should not be privately owned.

Socialization, education, information, motivation, mobilization.

Media should respond to needs of recipients.

Society can use censorship.

Marxist-Leninist view of society must be reflected in programming.

Supporting progressive (communist) movements.

Individuals as well as minority groups must be catered for by the media.

Basic assumptions:

Media should make a positive contribution to the national

development process.

Economic development and society should be more important than press freedom.

National, cultural and language issues should be high on the media's agenda.

Media should give preference to information about other developing countries that are geographically, culturally and politically akin to each other

Journalists have both responsibilities and liberties in obtaining and distributing information

State has the right to intervene by restricting and censoring the media. State subsidiaries and direct control is justifiable

Reaction against commercialization and monopolies

Against centralization and bureaucracies in public broadcasting

Developed societies

Internet future entertainment function

Much of the media produced today serves for the purpose of entertainment. Inform and educates on a latent and manifest level. The five internet entertainment aim and characteristic, it needs to own as below:

identity means entertainment focuses on human relations

ability means gives problem-solving possibilities

survival means awareness of eternal values (freeing from anxiety about destruction and death)

understanding means of reality and knowledge. shedding new light on reality (you're not alone)

From a rhetorical perspective the individual determines their interpretation of entertainment ,according to identity, social relation You can consider family series, police and action dramas or situation comedies, soap operas, game shows. From a behavioral perspective, entertainment is associated with the human ability to identify with others project and introject feelings but also with distancing from others.

Internet entertainment also makes a visual impact on the viewer, viewers become outsiders (not participants). Entertainment content (like any form of play) is always voluntary. The two parties on internet entertainment players may include: Introjection means viewer adopts feelings of other party. Projection = viewer projects feelings on other party (actors, characters) People are entertained when they produce their own opinions on these internet media situations.

Importance of understanding internet entertainment media effects: Strategic importance: to understand that messages – specific response – certain circumstance = strategically important in political, social awareness, marketing and advertising campaigns.

Scientific importance: contributes to the beneficial use of the media for the improvement of people's circumstance and society in general

Ethical importance: Responsibility of communication workers to know about the possible consequences of their work on the lives of people and society

Effects studies seek to discover describe and explain the internet entertainment media's specific effects on our behavior and thinking in a specific way. For example, the impact of pornography, violence and / or crime portrayed in and by the media on people's behavior. Internet can make use of mainly quantitative research techniques such as content analysis, survey research for entertainment aim.

CATEGORISING MEDIA AFFECTS:

Internet entertainment media ought not need to brings these message. They include: Media messages can affect our knowledge and thinking about something (e.g. thinking about racism), media messages can affect our feelings about something (e.g. child abuse, terrorism, violence.), media messages can affect our behavior towards something or someone (e.g. contribute to political rising against a government, org or group)

Internet entertainment media ought bring these message, such as , may have been planned to achieve a specific effect (e.g. HIV awareness campaign may be intended to warn people against disease) or not planned or intended (e.g. May teach certain people how to spread the disease, short term message exposure to single

message like one program – after that person forgets about it or intermediate message exposur to a series of related messages like a series on TV – (e.g. product campaign, stopping smoking) or long term exposure. Many exposures to related messages over time (e.g. media violence, pornography or awareness of environmental issues) may change our response or behavior over a long time.
An ongoing campaign to influence people's minds by focusing on negative aspects of an opponent / topic. Withholding positive or objective information Internet entertainment media campaigns ought include these elements, such as: An advertising campaign to promote a specific product or educational development. E.g. Topic people knew initially little or nothing about like global warming and its effects. Knowledge distribution concerns the media's contribution to cultural change, the media's contribution to Socialization.

- Reality defining – the media's interpretations of the realities of daily life and how we should understand them and avoiding Media violence – if the film or TV program causes violent behavior in an individual or amongst group.

Future internet entertainment media needs to bring these long-term benefits to internet players. They may include as below:
Media focus (a newspaper or different newspapers by example)– repeatedly and consistent and over a long period, focus on a specific topic equals to changes in beliefs, attitudes and behavior. Focus attention and produce messages on specific problems or issues (E.g. race, discrimination, the environment, social habits, crime, divorce, style, sex, politics). Over extended period of time focus stays and presentation corroborate each other. Individuals become aware of these messages, and a growing.
In general, children will apply internet to play online games. However, online games will bring both advantages and disadvantages as below:
The Internet has been a gaming medium for almost as long as it has existed, as early users quickly adapted email and newsgroup technology to create online versions of classic board games or

roleplaying games. Since the early 2000s, the growth of broadband Internet has brought new generations of gamers online; in fact, you can't play some modern games such as Titanfall offline at all. While there are a lot of advantages to online gaming, it does have a seedy underbelly.

Internet can help children to make friend when they entertain from internet. More than anything else, online games have brought players together, forging people with a shared interest into a community. Whether cooperative or competitive, online gaming makes it much easier for gamers to play with their friends or make new ones. Guildmates can play together in an online role-playing game or sports rivals test their skills even though they live thousands of miles apart. Friendships can develop in online games between people who would never have met otherwise. Recent research even shows that children who play online games are more likely to develop positive attitudes toward people from other countries and cultures.

But, internet can also encourage bad behavior

Game makers and community moderators do their best to limit this kind of behavior, but it still plagues some online communities. Luckily, most games offer a way to ignore or mute other players if you are encountering a barrage of insults.

Connection Problems

Modern online gaming is usually a very smooth experience, but the technology still has its limits. Small delays in internet connections can result in "lag," a delay between when you press a button and the action occurs in the game. In input-sensitive games like first-person shooters or fighting games, this small delay is the difference between victory and defeat.

Cost

Internet connection charges can quickly add up when playing online: Gamers whose ISPs impose data caps may find themselves using up their bandwidth quickly. Players may also have to pay monthly for online accounts or spend money per item on in-game purchases, and the costs can add up quickly for unsuspecting players.

Competitive Communities

Competitive gamers are among the biggest beneficiaries of online gaming. Previously, most players' knowledge of the competitive scene was limited to a local group such as an arcade or a university gaming club. Online gaming -- aided by other online tools such as Twitch and YouTube -- has made it possible for competitive players to share strategies and analyze gameplay like never before, raising the standard of play to a new level and creating an entirely new industry of professional competitive gaming. However, there is a downside to this boom, as new players can often find the high level of play demanded by competitive gamers intimidating, and may not even attempt to play online.

Thus, future internet entertainment ought not need concern on playing games aspect, it ought apply to entertainment media knowledge or message aspect, if our society can expect our generation develop successfully, because when they apply internet to learn new and useful knowledge for entertainment aim more than playing games to waste time aim. Then, we shall have many internet new knowledge young people who can apply their new knowledge from internet learning to attribute our society.

What is Internet learning function

The Services are used by the people to get information, do online works, discussions, e-mailing, video chatting, voice calling, social activities, news channels, online booking and many other hundred and thousand terms that we use with the help of internet. In every country there are many companies that provide the services of net in different rates. There get benefits from full functions you need to have a laptop, mobile or PC. All above these which will need any internet users to learn in order to achieve their consumption or playing or entertainment or learning aim.

Advantages / Merits / Uses / Benefits of Internet

● Online Shopping

Now today's the trend of online shopping is growing up very fast. Users have now the facility of shop everything what they want without going outside to stores and super markets.

Benefits for Students Studies

You are a student and you miss the lecture. Don't worry internet helps students to find notes, essay, lectures, guidelines and more than points related to your subject are available in your books.

Book Tickets online

In the race of technology and companies are giving best services to their users. And almost all the airlines are providing advantages to their customer to buy the tickets online on internet. So people are no need to go to the agency or airline office.

Learn Online From Videos

Internet is the solution of many problems. If you face any problem in your mobile, laptop, cars, television etc. You can easily find the solution on the screen with the help of video providing website. Mostly used websites for videos upload and downloads are YouTube, Dailymotion, tunepk, viemo and etc.

Play Online Games

People fond of video games are easily access to download multiple games. Also can play online games with the help of internet connection. Without it you can't play online either can't download.

Entertainment

Every day new movies and music lunched in every country almost. People how are fond to watch movies or listen music. They can easily find latest music and movies on Internet and can download it and also watch it online.

E-mailing

Government Departments, Private Organization, Businesses, NGOs, School, Colleges and Universities etc. And many other departments and peoples are using the e-mail services. And I'll say that without e-mail conversation half of word would be stop work. Because big projects, secret information and files are shared through e-mails and this service is not possible without Internet Connection.

Results and Roll No

Students of Universities and Colleges now even the students of

Schools are easily see their results on internet. To access to the result you must need to put the right roll no in the search bar of school or college website.

Jobs

Hundreds of mobile application, and thousands of website in every country. In their national language provide the services to the jobless peoples to find the jobs on Internet related to their experience and criteria.

Bank Accounts

Money in your bank account is now same like money in your pocket. Yes you can login to your account and make online transactions either bank is open or close.

Buy and Sell

If you have second hand or new bike, car, clothes, shoes, jewelry, mobile or laptop etc. You can place an add to website and easily can sell on reasonable price as compare to market. You can also buy same like this by contacting the selling person.

Earn Money On Internet

Create a professional website or create a channel on video website. Run for little time and place an advertisement on your website or channel and earn money through net. You can also earn money by affiliate marketing.

Hire Peoples for Work

Hire online people to get advantages to complete your assignments, petty works, designs, data entry works etc. there are several famous website where you can easily hire a person for your work. Fiver and Upwork are good example of it.

However, online learning may bring these disadvantage to influence student individual learning attitude or learning emotion, I shall indicate reasons as below:

In recent years, internet addiction has been a world-wide problem among the youth. Many of them may sit in front of the computer to play online game; chat with others for the whole day without resting. Those prolonged activities bring a lot of destructive effect to them both. They apply internet to play more than apply this high technological media tool for learning aim usually. Internet can be very constructive, but we must be conscious how much time we spend on it on a daily basis. People are addicted to the internet since they do not control the amount of time they spend on it. It is important to have other interests apart from the internet.

Today, surfing the Web has become a hobby as social and marketable as bar hopping or going to the movies. As the web has become a part of mainstream life, some mental health professionals have noted that a percentage of people using the web do so in a compulsive and out-of-control manner. In Japan (Aril 2010), a 30-year-old man who is addicted to internet killed his father and his 1 year-old niece because of his father terminated the contract of internet broadband. He then set up a fire and burnt his house. In this case, 2 people died and 3 people injured. This phenomenon of obsessive Internet use has been termed 'Internet Addiction' based on its similarity to common addictions such as smoking, drinking, and gambling. Internet Addiction has even been championed as an actual disorder, notably by some psychologists. Nevertheless, at this time the true nature of Internet Addiction is not yet determined.

Because the Internet is used by many people as a normal part of their career or education, knowing how to separate excessive from normal use becomes difficult and cannot using simple measures such as amount of time spent online in a given period. Most fundamental in distinguishing normal from problem Internet use is the experience of compulsion to use the net. Normal users, no matter how heavy their usage, do not need to get online and do not neglect their occupational duties or their relationships with family and friends to get online.

Mental health professionals are split as to whether Internet addiction is real or not. No one disputes that some people use the Internet in an obsessive manner even to a point where it interferes with their ability to function at work and in social relationships. What is doubtful is whether people can become addicted to the Internet itself, or rather to the stimulation and information that the web provides. The argument surrounding Internet Addiction is precisely whether people become addicted to the net itself, or to the stimulation to be had via the net, such as online gambling, pornography or even simple communication with others via chat and blogs.

Some psychologists do not consider in addiction to the Internet itself, but rather in addiction to stimulation that the Internet provides. They propose that new Internet users often show an initial fascination with the innovation of the Web, but eventually lose interest and reduce their time spent online back to a normal, healthy amount. Those abuser who do go on to show obsessive Internet utilization, for the most part become compulsive only with considering to particular types of information to be had online, mainly often gambling, pornography, chat room or shopping sites. This is not an addiction to the Internet itself, but rather to risk-taking, sex, socializing or shopping. In real meaning, the main addictive characteristic of the Internet is its capability to enable instant and relatively social stimulation. "Addicted" Internet users are addicted to a favored kind of social stimulation and not to the Internet itself, although it is also true that the Internet has made it easier and more convenient for someone to develop such a compulsion.

Why peoples especially youth have internet addition? There are some reasons to explain it. By Internal Factors-The background of growth, the family is believed to have a fundamental influence on the developing child. A caregiver who is emotionally and physically available is essential for healthy child and adolescent development. Besides, dysfunctional caregiving, lack of positive parenting skills, and poor family management are strongly associated with substance use and delinquency in youth. Therefore, the youth growth up in poor family will seek alternative to fulfil their psychological needs, it is compensation. The level of compensation is depending on the individual factors such as the degree of self control, emotional control, ability of problem solving, anxiety management. When over compensation, addition will occur. There are some reasons that people choose internet for compensation.

From social learning, when adolescents' strong developmental needs, such as personal identity, autonomy, and relationships with peers may not be fulfilled through physical activities, they may then shed social inhibitions, also when they are dissatisfied with their leisure time, they may be motivated to seek excitement and pleasure from cyberspace and therefore raise their level of Internet addiction. Besides, encourage of society and the common use of Internet activities raise the level of Internet addiction. Furthermore, the traditional activities are perceived to be boring and fails to satisfy expected optimal experience, the youth may be motivated to seek another alternative-the Internet. Internet not only fulfills youth's psychological needs but also entertainment needs. Lastly, Internet dependency was burden and the youth become habituated by using.

Internet addiction is not recognized as a formal mental health disorder. However, mental health professionals who have written about the subject note symptoms or behaviors that, when present in sufficient numbers, may indicate problematic use. These include:

Obsession with the Internet: User often thinks about the Internet while he or she is offline.

Loss of control: Addicted users feel unable or unwilling to get up from the computer and walk away. They sit down to check e-mail or look up a bit of information, and end up staying online for hours.

Inexplicable sadness or moodiness when not online: Reliance on any substance often causes mood-altering side effects when the addicted user is separated from the substance on which he or she depends.

Distraction (Using the Internet as an anti-depressant): One common symptom of many Internet addicts is the compulsion to cheer one's self up by surfing the Web.

Dishonesty in regard to Internet use: Addicts may end up lying to employers or family members about the amount of time they spend online, or find other ways to conceal the depth of their involvement with the Internet.

Loss of boundaries or inhibitions: While this often pertains to romantic or sexual boundaries, such as sharing sexual fantasies online or participating in cyber sex, inhibitions can also be financial or social. Online gambling sites can cause addicts to blow more money than they would in a real-life casino because users never actually see their money won or lost, so it is easier to believe the money is not real. Chat rooms can incite users to reveal secrets they would not reveal in face-to-face or phone conversations because of the same separation from reality. Also, addicted users are much more likely to commit crimes while online (e.g., 'hacking') than non-addicts. Creation of virtual intimate relationships with other Internet users: Web-based relationships often cause those involved to spend excessive amounts of time online, attempting to make connections and date around the Net. Loss of a significant relationship due to Internet use: When users spend too much time on the Web, they often neglect their personal relationships. Over time, such relationships may fail as partners simply refuse to be treated badly and break off from relations with the addicted individual.

Internet Addiction is not an official disorder, and many mental health professionals are not certain if it ever should be considered a real disorder. Nevertheless, compulsive Internet use is a serious problem for some people, and there are methods that can be helpful in alleviating this problem. Discussion below will describe some of these methods. Internet addiction is a problem of compulsive stimulation, much like drug addiction. Because of this similarity, well studied treatment procedures known to be useful for helping drug addicts towards recovery are adapted for use with Internet addicts when the need arises. The techniques we describe below are drawn from a popular school of therapy known as 'cognitive-behavioral' therapy. Cognitive behavioral forms of therapy are well studied and known to be helpful as applied to many different mental and behavioral difficulties. They are also very practical and focus directly on reducing out of control 'addict' behaviors, and preventing relapse. They are not the only valid forms of therapy, however.

In treating drug addiction, frequently the goal of therapy is abstainence. An alcoholic, for example, is often best off if he or she ceases to drink alcohol entirely and to maintain a sober lifestyle. While this makes sense for a drug like alcohol which we might argue is a at best a luxury recreational indulgence and not a necessity, but it doesn't necessarily make sense for Internet over-usage. Much like the telephone, the Internet has become an essential part of modern business. To ask people to not use the Internet at all could be a significant burden for them. Instead of abstainence, then, a reasonable goal for Internet addiction therapy is a reduction in total use of the net. Because Internet addicts by definition will have difficulty moderating their use on their own, therapy techniques can be employed to help them to become more motivated to reduce their use, and to become more conscious of how they get into trouble with the Internet.

Motivational Interviewing may be employed to assess how motivated Internet addict may be to change their behavior and to help addicts to increase their motivation to make a lasting change. To accomplish the latter, a therapist may help addicts to develop genuine empathy for the people who are hurt by their addiction (e.g., family and friends, employers, etc.). By helping addicts to see how their actions affect others they care about or are dependent on economically, therapists can help increase addicts motivation to change.

Setting up (healthy) rewards that patients can earn when goals have been met for an agreed upon amount of time. Since one of the main draws of the Internet is the secrecy it appears to give, sharing online experiences in the context of offline relationships may discourages a user from 'hiding' in the Internet. Sharing progress in a group therapy session, with a therapist, or with a family member can help motivation to cut back on Internet time.

With regard to Internet addiction, it is possible to install computer programs designed to monitor where someone surfs and how long they spend there to provide an accurate and objective report of someone's surfing behavior. PC software will monitor the kinds and number of websites a person uses and the amount of time spent Web surfing or checking e-mail. Such programs can help compulsive Internet users supervise their own Internet use, but only if they are installed so as to be hard to tamper with.

What Are The Advantages And Disadvantages Of Online Learning?

Learning is often considered to be a normal part of working and personal life. Both learning for achieving a job as well as for achieving knowledge should not be neglected. Online environment is changing continuously and it represents a great opportunity for learning. It is very important to discover how to learn using all available communication channels and choosing the ones that best suit a person's style of filtering the information. Nowadays, online learning turns out to be more and more practiced. Many traditional universities started to share their courses online for free. It represents an easy and comfortable method to achieve knowledge in almost every field, from law and accounting, to human sciences, such as psychology and sociology or history. Online learning is a great alternative to traditional universities, especially for people who can't afford the time and money to take real courses. But what are the advantages and disadvantages of online learning?

Advantages Of Online Learning

Although many people still consider traditional universities as the best way to achieve knowledge and get a diploma, online learning proves to be a great alternative. Students have the chance to study in their own time and especially for free. It represents a great way to study many fields and to boost the level of self-motivation. Online learning is so effective because students can finish their homework quickly, and there is more time left for hobbies or for finding a job. An access to all resources of a traditional course helps participants learn wherever they are, leaving them the freedom to choose the time for study. With basically an Internet connection, a person can attend different courses. Among the advantages of online learning there are the responsibility and self-discipline of students.

Disadvantages Of Online Learning

Only in a small group a person can develop properly. At school, students learn how to make friends, be patient, get rid of disappointment, and especially to compete. Competition between colleagues can be very stimulating and students will only benefit from it. Online learning cannot offer human interaction. Another disadvantage refers to the fact that online courses cannot cope with thousands of students that try to join discussions. Also, online learning can be difficult, if it is meant for disciplines that involve practice.

In conclusion, online learning should be seen as a complement and extension of classical forms of learning. Not even the best online course can fully replace the personal contact with a teacher, or the human relationships that develop in a group. So, traditional classes shouldn't be replaced with online

What is internet for searching information function

The Internet is important for a huge variety of reasons, and it affects and facilitates nearly every aspect of modern life. The Internet is extremely important in many fields, from education and healthcare to business and government. The Internet has had an enormous impact on education, streamlining access to information and making it easier for individuals to engage in online learning. Distance education programs make it easier for students from a variety of backgrounds to attend classes remotely, cutting down the need for travel and reducing the resources required for education.

The Internet has also made access to information and communication far easier. Rather than searching the library, users can access vast amounts of information from home computers. Internet access has a huge impact on businesses, allowing employees to work remotely from home and communicate more efficiently. Healthcare is another field greatly affected by the advent of the Internet. Improvements in online connectivity and communication technology allow physicians much greater access to medical resources. Doctors in rural areas can also use the Internet to communicate with experts all over the world, improving the quality of patients' diagnoses and treatments. Politics and government are another area in which the Internet is important. Government organizations use the Internet to improve organization and communication, and voters can go online to gain more information about current issues. According to Web Junction, 54 percent of adults went online to get information about the 2010 U.S. midterm elections.

Most information is found on the Internet by utilizing search engines. A search engine is a web service that uses web robots to query millions of pages on the Internet and creates an index of those web pages. Internet users can then use these services to find information on the Internet. When searching for information on the Internet, keep the below things in mind. If you are searching for multiple common words, such as computer and help, it is a good idea to place quotes around the full search to get better results. For example, type "computer help" as your search criteria. This trick can also be used in parts of your search query. For example, Microsoft "computer help" would search for anything containing 'Microsoft' and that also has "computer help" together. Finally, you can also do multiple words surrounded in quotes. For example, "Microsoft Windows" and "computer help" would refine your results even more. Many search engines will strip out common words they refer to as stop words for each search that is performed. For example, instead of searching for why does my computer not boot, the search engine would search for computer and boot. To help prevent these stop words from being stripped out, surround the search with quotes.

The Internet is a very powerful worldwide instrument, which serves as a good source for research work and learning. It generates current information, facts-finding, and is the most outstanding invention in the area of communication in the history of human race. The Internet has been very useful to mankind in the aspect of learning and research development. In due course, this essay emphasizes on details of advantages and disadvantages of the Internet in relation to research work.

In conclusion, internet can bring searching information advantages

and disadvantages to compare other channels as below:
Advantages:
The Internet eases of communication to the researchers; because it serves as a guidance and original source of information. It is very easy to access and at the same time saves time thereby allowing an individual to manager his/her resources better and effectively. Additionally, the Internet is very convenient because an individual can easily carry out a research work at home with much comfort and convenience. The internet is a valuable search tool and has been informative for academic research, as it helps significantly to improve research skills, and makes learning visual and easy to follow.
Comparatively Inexpensive and Quick Dispersion of Information:
The Internet creates a comparatively inexpensive avenue for releasing information and articles. Subsequently, several organizations and individuals can now circulate information to millions of users. In due course, researchers could assess and make use of this circulated information and articles for their work, thereby giving them a broader idea and knowledge in their work.
Additionally, there is a spontaneous dispersion of information to various users of the internet when such information is being added to a web site. As regards this, millions of users including researchers would browse through these information and subsequently use them for their work. Hence the web is then regarded as a paragon medium for disseminating information because it removes the time wasting in between publishing content and making it available to users.
Wealth of Information:
Furthermore, the Internet is a wealth of information and very advantageous in various reasons; students delve into the Internet to gather lots of very useful academic information for research purposes; and the information contained on the Internet can be useful for academic research. It is a potential research tool and opens up a new and comprehensive source of information.
In another development, information is probably the biggest

advantage internet is offering to the users. The Internet is an apparent treasure trove of information. Any kind of information on any topic under the sun is available on the Internet.

Sending E-mail Messages and Receiving Feedbacks:

With the help of the Internet the user could send e-mails to colleagues, friends, co-workers etc, either to get more information from them or pass on the acquired information to them. In view of this the Internet could be regarded as a powerful content publishing tool because there are some application software embedded in the Internet that enable such transmission and transfer of information from one user to another. Consequently, these applications will allow and assist the researcher to develop content for the World Wide Web by simply saving as an HTML file.

Disadvantages:

Having discussed the advantages of the Internet for academic research it is worthy to mention some of its disadvantages. One of the disadvantages of the Internet is that it provides a huge amount of information thereby causing information overload. In due course, one can easily get confused with this infinite amount of titles, texts and abstracts. And because of the overwhelming information available on the Internet, one must be cautious about information obtained.

There are no standards, that is, no process to check information accurately. Most information in the Internet does not go through a review process. Anyone can publish on the web, without passing the content through an editor. Pages might be written by an expert on the topic, or even a child, or a disgruntled contributor. Therefore, getting information from book or from various other printed sources in the library can guarantee that it is of high standard and peer reviewed.

Additionally, it can be observed that with a large amount of information freely available on the internet, theft of personal information and misuse of this information is in abundance. In this regard from time to time people use someone's information and research materials and pass it off as their own work. Also,

Spamming, which is the process of sending unwanted or junk e-mails in bulk, which provide no purpose and consequently hinder the entire system. This in due course is regarded as an illegal activity resulting to frustrate people. As regards this, a researcher could check his e-mail to obtain some materials for his work; only to get disappointed when noticed that the e-mail was a junk. The issue of spamming extends to commercial advertising, frequently for dubious products, get-rich-quick, or semi-legal services.

Furthermore, another disadvantage of the Internet is virus threat. In this regard, Virus is a program that interrupts the normal functioning of the computer systems. Computers that are attached to internet are more likely to be attacked by virus. In due course, this attack could result to hard disk crashing, thereby causing a big disaster on the computer. On the other hand, some unprincipled individuals have been successful in creating viruses and links that once clicked can automatically transmit ones personal e-mail addresses and other details to certain parties and even the person's bank account details in some extreme cases.

Additionally, another disadvantage of the Internet for academic research is that, it is not arranged according to system and no index format. Information on the Internet is not organized; for example too many web pages for any single directory services and fees are often charged for access to specialized information.

In conclusion, irrespective of the fact that the Internet has some numerous disadvantages, it can be understood that it is still very useful to mankind as in helps in medical research works and subsequent inventions, as well as produce some good interactive entertainment and multimedia. Hence, man needs the Internet to keep life going. Man asserts that, the Internet is considered not simply as a technological tool, but as a wholly new constructed environment with its own codes of practice.

Information security threats

New security threats are emerging every day from malware programs that can be inadvertently installed on a user's machine, to phishing attempts that deceive employees into giving up confidential information, to viruses, worms, and strategic identity theft attempts. Sometimes the threat that attacks the information in organizations is difficult to handles. It is because the protection programs that installed in the computer system to protect the data are not appropriately function or not good enough.

Difficulties in manage information security because of do not the proper qualification in information security.

Sometimes organizations do not take seriously about hiring employees based on their qualification. This is because there are organizations that hiring employees for the information security manager but it is doesn't match with his qualification or skill that he have about information security. So, it is difficult for that staff to protect the organizations data with proper protection. This will makes other attackers easier to attacks and stole the information if the employees don't have skill or knowledge on how to protect the confidential data.

Conclusion

Information security is crucial in organization. All information stored in the organization should be kept secure. Information security will be defined as the protection of data from any threats of virus. The information security in important in the organization because it can protect the confidential information, enables the organization function, also enables the safe operation of application implemented on the organization's Information Technology system, and information is an asset for an organization. Even thought the information is important in organization, there are several challenges to protect and manages the information as well. One of challenges faced in an organization is the lack of understanding on important of information security. When employees is lack of information security knowledge in term of keeping their information, the organization is easy to being attacks by hackers or another threats that try to stole or get the organization confidential information. So it is crucial and important to all staff in an organization to have knowledge and understanding about the importance information security practice in an organization to protect the confidential data when they need to gather any information from internet channel.

What is internet for online office function

There are lots of compelling reasons to work remotely — but some business leaders and employment experts argue that it's better to work onsite. So, online working mode is same to virtual teams — geographically scattered colleagues who use high-tech communication — are now common in many organizations. Some of those team members are remote workers and some still work onsite, in the traditional office. But if remote work is indeed going to kill office work, get ready for a tough time. Remote work can be hard, both for workers and their managers. Even if the employer has a good flexible working policy and the employee has the right skills for remote work, there are downsides to working from home. Why all the office jobs will disappear in possible? Here are examples of how onsite work is replaced by remote work. They include :

1: Working onsite fosters innovation

It's all very well offering flexible working improvements like remote work to employees. Online working can bring these working benefits , such as Some of the best decisions and insights come from hallway and cafeteria discussions, meeting new people, and impromptu team meetings, they can finish from internet channel.

2: Onsite workers are easier to manage

In addition to the regular employee management that a team leader deals with, remote workers carry plenty of extra baggage that needs managing. Having remote workers, "creates a potential problem for managers used to having their team in the same room as them," said Jonathan Swan, of work/life balance charity Working Families.

3: Some employees can telecommute

Some employees can learn certain combination of skills to successfully work from home easily. Also, remote workers must show better discipline, communication skills, and punctuality than their office-bound colleagues. In other words, they have to run faster just to keep up.

4: Communication is easier in the online environment

Some employees can feel easy to communicate in a video conference? Can you share donuts using Windows Messenger? And what happens when you communicate less effectively with your peers? They trust you less. Remote workers must be even more contactable than their office-based colleagues or trust goes out the window.

5: Office work is bore and some jobs can be done remotely

It is important for young people to have a sense of belonging and that they needed to know the rules and boundaries between work and play before taking advantage of remote working. In Europe, where many employees have a legal right to be considered for flexible work, only 18% actually telework (telework is defined as remote work using IT). In Germany it's 12% —and those workers are mainly highly qualified, such as managers, academics, lawyers, journalists, engineers and teachers.

6: Flexible hours are popular with businesses to remote work

A CBI (Confederation of British Industry) employment trends survey said, "Five years ago, just 13% of firms offered teleworking for employees in at least certain roles some of the time, but now nearly six in ten (59%) do so." Sounds like a lot, right? But just because remote work options are available doesn't mean that's the type of flexible working all the cool companies are doing. Andy Lake, editor of flexible work resource Flexibility, said that more than 90% of companies offered flexible working of some kind, but that this was mostly flexible hours and part-time working.

Future online working model brings traditional office working model to be reformed

Office work is alive, well, and adapted to the needs of modern organizations. Traditional onsite working is going nowhere.

Pros and Cons of working from home vs. working from the office

If your job offered you an option of working from home or working in the office – would you take it? Would you be more productive working in sweatpants vs your usual business casual? Would you have more time for you family if you do not have to spend two hours commuting every day? Would you miss the corporate environment or would you enjoy solitude? Can video conferences, phone calls and remote access really make you feel like you are part of the office when you are not physically present? If you are confused about what option is right for you – here are a few things to think about.

The positive side of working from home

It can bring time saved , it means that the online working can do more himself time at home. The biggest advantage of working from home is that you save a lot of time commuting back and forth to work. This may mean some extra shuteye or the opportunity to not skip breakfast in the morning. You can spend extra time with your children or spouse, read the newspaper instead of sitting in traffic. Start off your day in a calm fashion instead of being stressed and rushed to get to the office. Taking time for yourself is often very difficult, you may find that having extra me time in the mornings will make you happy and therefore a more productive employee.

You are in control of your working environment

Another benefit of working from home is that you have the ability to create your working environment. With no cubical walls defining your space you have the freedom to choose your office location, the perfect corner office perhaps?

You define your hours

With no time clock, you can start and stop your day as you please. You can get started a little earlier or take a few extra minutes during lunch. As long as you work your required hours and get your job done there is no harm is shifting your schedule a bit. For example, Video conferences only show you from the waste up. If the mood felt right you could wear a suit shirt and shorts or pajama bottoms. And what about days when you don't have to video chat with anyone from your office. Working in sweatpants and pajamas becomes completely possible.

The negative side of working from home

Solitary confinement?

Many people find that working from home is like solitary confinement. We all crave human interactions and sometimes video conferences and phone calls wont satisfy this need. Even though you can get in touch with your office, you no longer have the constant support of your colleagues and supervisors.

Technical issues

Sure, when everything works – it is fantastic, but if your Internet cuts out or you loose access to your company's intranet, you may be unable to do your job. Most companies have tech support designed to handle off-site employees, but you will never receive the same level of support as you would in an office setting.

How disciplined are you?

Have you ever thought that working from home also takes discipline? It is very easy to switch to surfing the web or home chores that need to be done. When you work from home you may actually find it harder to focus and get your work done. When you work from home your work day never ends. Since it starts and stops in the same place you may find yourself working later into the evening not realizing what time it is. Some people find that when they work from home that their jobs starts to bleed into their personal life. That while they assumed working from home would give them more freedom that it in fact has caused them to work longer hours and sometimes on the weekends.

The positive side of working in an office

So are you asking yourself, if I don't have to get dressed and spend an hour commuting back and forth everyday why would I want to? Well, have you ever thought how positive and rewarding working in an office can be?

Motivation for career growth

When you work in an office environment, you have supervision and restrictions, but you also have knowledge and support from your bosses and colleagues. Being around intelligent people might motivate you. A competitive environment might encourage you to preform better, helping you to excel in your field and ultimately your place in the company.

Immediate feedback

If you are in an office and you have a question – you can stand up and walk over to someones desk and ask them. You can bring them to your desk to show them something on your computer screen. You can have a meeting that doesn't involve videoconferencing. You can collaborate with your colleagues on a project without a digital whiteboard, you can use an actual whiteboard.

Social network

You may find that you benefit personally from being in an office. Having a social life is very important and for many their coworkers are their social network. Having lunch with your coworkers, catching up with one another, going out for happy hour, these are all positive and rewarding activities. Again, when you are happy and satisfied you are a more productive employee.

The negative side of working in an office the commute

One of the biggest advantages of working from home is in turn the biggest disadvantage of working in an office. You can spend upwards of three hours commuting back and forth to work everyday. Traffic, congestion and wasted time all add up to stress. Have you ever found yourself running to work flustered that your boss would be angry with you for being late, even if the circumstances were out of your control? Have you ever had to leave work early to make it to your child's soccer game, dance recital or a PTA meeting? The extra time it takes to get to and from work is time wasted that could be spent in a much more productive manner. If your office is like most offices it consists of a few corner offices, a wall of windows, and a sea of cubicles. It is very possible that you may not be able to tell the weather or if it is day or night from where you sit in the office. Sun light increases happiness and indirectly your productivity. It is an essential part of life. You wouldn't choose to live in a home with no windows would you?

Some people are happier working in an office and some people are happier working from home. You have to weigh your options and decide what is best for you. Can you be disciplined enough to work from home? Will you be happy without the daily support of your co-workers? Both options have their advantages and disadvantages. Only you can decide what is the best option for you. Otherwise, some online working people give their opinions, they indicate that they work from home every day, as my employer mandates it for all paid staff due to financial reasons. Great for work life balance and saves on commute time, road tolls and petrol. But it does feel isolating at times and I miss the collaboration with the rest of my team, though we have our monthly team meetings back at our headquarters! And yes, on those rare occasions when my computer or internet connection is not cooperating with me, it can be depressing as we don't have easy access to IT support. On those days when I feel like working from home is doing my head in and I start feeling the loneliness creep in, I head to any of my local cafes with good Wifi connection, or even my local library. They agree – it's not for everyone, but as long as the work gets done, I don't see any issues with it.

That's what facilities managers and office managers around the world are asking themselves about the office spaces they're responsible for organizing. How can they set up a space that's not just a place to shelter all your employees, but one that's a strategic tool for productivity, collaboration, and growth?cWhat makes an office environment great is different for every company. A lot of it has to do with a company's culture and how employees there like to work. And the right office environment can set employees up with the right situation and motivation to tackle big, important projects (like getting inbound certified, perhaps?)Want to get inspired by examples of what your workplace could look like?

Why are changing the Workplace when online office working model will be popular ?

Thanks to wireless internet, laptops, and tablets, employees are finding they don't necessarily need to be chained to a single desk. Instead, they can move around their space more, technology in tow. And some companies have taken this to the next level by eliminating personal desks and opting for a configuration called "hot desking." Hot desking simply means no one in the office has an assigned desk or seating area. Instead, when you come in to work in the morning, you can sit anywhere you please -- from open tables or desks set up with cables and monitors, to more public spaces like couches and chairs. For this to work, a company should take special care to create spaces in the office that can easily be reconfigured for different tasks and evolving teams.

Some companies CEO believe that they don't want our employees sitting in one chair all day, because that's not good for them and it's not good for collaboration. We just get these really great intersections of people and ideas ... Suddenly and randomly, we'll have these conversations with people from finance, legal, design, and you get these collaborations that wouldn't otherwise occur. They love how flexible it is, and that there are always different people sitting at my desk. It makes me feel more in touch with my co-workers and what's going on in the company."

But be aware that hot desking may not be an effective way to create movement in the office. One study found that when people didn't have an assigned desk, they didn't move around more; instead, they would find a place to work and then stay there for the rest of the day. So, while interaction among employees did increase by 17% in the study, the number of individuals‘ encounters during the day actually dropped by an average of 14%. As a result, team communication actually dropped by 45%. If you like the idea of creating movement in your office but don't want to eliminate assigned seating altogether, you might try playing "musical chairs" every few months, where you keep teams together but change their assigned seating area every few months.

For international office in Zurich, Switzerland, and use desks that can be reconfigured to work individually or collaboratively. Desks there fit together like puzzle pieces and can be moved, reworked, and reattached as employees see fit -- a nod to the values of modern office design, which include mobility, flexibility, and collaboration. Another alternative to help encourage spontaneous collaboration among your employees is designing your space to allow for "overlap zones," which make it more likely your employees will run into each other. How do your employees move throughout the day? Where do they go? What kind of spaces would cause them to run into each other more frequently?

Research from the University of Michigan showed that when scientists worked in a space where they ran into one another -- in areas known as “zonal overlap" -- they were more likely to collaborate. The data suggests that creating opportunities for unplanned interactions among employees both inside and outside the organization actually improves performance.

Music Rooms innovation

One way to boost employee productivity at the office is to foster a positive company culture. To give employees a place to blow off steam at work, why not add a music room to the mix? For the musically inclined, going into the company music room to playing music alone or with coworkers is one way to do it. (And for the non-musically inclined, let’s hope that music room is super soundproofed.)

A "Superdesk" innovation

Designing an office space around the "open office" concept is one thing. But what about creating a shared desk for your company’s entire staff? For employees who want to work in a quieter space or have more private discussions, the desk lifts into large arches that have seats built underneath them.

Researchers have found that adding plants and greenery in an office can help increase employee productivity by 15%. “A green office communicates to employees that their employer cares about them and their welfare,” said Psychology Professor Alex Haslam, who co-authored the study. "Office landscaping helps the workplace become a more enjoyable, comfortable and profitable place to be.” Some companies have even started investing in installing plants and greenery around the office help make their employees happier and healthier (and boosting productivity at the same time). For example, Google’s office in Tel Aviv, Israel has an indoor orange grove that turns an otherwise normal, collaborative space into a relaxing area that makes you feel like you're sitting outside on a park bench.

Thus, online communication systems are emerging as real-time communication tools for individuals, students and business professionals and it can bring above innovations to traditional office working designing environment change. These systems are a perfect blend of video, audio and computer technology that allows people to connect in real time irrespective of their geographical locations and time zones.

Undoubtedly, digital conferencing makes interaction exciting for users at different physical locations by providing them access to high-quality sound and full-motion video effects. However, research shows a two-sided report of the impact of these online communication systems.

Top Benefits of Online Communication can include as below:

1. Cost effective compared to physical meeting

Web conference services are cost effective in every possible angle, as the services would be in need of a computer or a mobile along with internet connectivity. To a physical conference, you have to spare time, money to travel, cost to stay and so on. A digital connectivity has given huge benefits regarding using web conference option on a regular basis.

2. Easy connectivity from every place in the world

online conferencing is not a baby technology anymore, where the connection was never stable. The web conferencing technology has improved to a great extent and provides flawless connectivity from any part of the world. You can use the online conferencing services for both official and personal purposes, as there are multiple numbers of applications that you can use to initiate a virtual meeting.

3. Best to use in different devices and gadgets

You can do online conferencing both on the computer and on mobile phones. Most of the smartphones give out an option for users to have a web meeting on a regular basis without paying any cost. As technology is advancing at a rapid speed, some of the applications are available free of cost both in mobile and in the computer, which can be used to make long distance calls without paying a dime.

4. Increase productivity and efficiency

The efficiency of a business house depends more or less on the ease of communication and smooth flow of information between employees working at different levels. Though interaction mostly takes place via e-mail, phone or instant messaging system but visually interactive video-conferencing is providing a better alternative. It gives vital visual images that enable employees and customers to interpret and collaborate properly over a long distance. As a result, decisions are taken faster, projects execute on-time and productivity increases.

5. Long-term competitive advantage

Video-conferencing gives users multiple options for securing competitive advantage. When employees or business associates interact over video, they can share messages more rapidly resulting in more wise decisions that minimize both the time and price required to promote new services and products. Through the technical support of the videoconferencing company, business owners get an opportunity to leverage video effects and create more valuable and personal bonding with the customers and build up a loyalty which is far beyond the capacities of traditional phone conferencing system.

6. Ultimate support for environmental protection

Since the videoconferencing system works on green technology, business organizations can be prevented from emitting energy and increasing the level of carbon in the environment. Thus, interaction over video has made every small and medium sized business organization environment conscious and urged them to stick to environment-friendly communication methods. With wide scale availability of tools that make on-demand production of live video footages possible anywhere in the world, students, customers, and employees get a chance to become part of an environmental initiative.

However, web conferences can also bring this disadvantages as below:

1. Time-consuming and costly

One of the major disadvantages of web conference call is that detail planning is essential for its success. The people engaged in the conference call need to have high discipline and high level of concentration. For an effective conference call the web cam, microphone and other gadgets need to be in proper position and in good working condition. Failure in any one of the key gadgets can lead to the total failure of the conference call.

2. Ineffective

There are some human ways of communicating that do not translate very well over a distance, such as an eye contact. When you sit in the same room with someone and listen to a speech or presentation you will make eye contact and they will judge who is paying attention by looking around the room. Much of this contact is not easily delivered through a webcam.

In conclusion, the advantages and disadvantages of video conferencing have to be weighed against your purpose and whether there will be something valuable lost through this technology that you don't want to give up. ezTalks is a one-stop video and audio conferencing solution provider offering a wide range of quality online communication services. The company offers cost effective call solutions which will require an IP or ISDN network connection, conference equipment (camera, microphone, monitor, and speakers), a codec and an audio system for being functional. The recent developments in audio and video conferencing technology have made it far more productive and engaging than conventional teleconferencing.

Cross-team collaboration in the workplace is a critical aspect when it comes to performance and productivity on any project. It not only inspires innovative approaches to a project but also leads to quick decision making. With the growth of video conferencing systems and software, employees can now collaborate from anywhere at any time using minimal resources.

The use of such video conference software as ezTalks Cloud Meeting has really revolutionized the way businesses collaborate online. But just like any other office process out there, online collaboration comes with a set of advantages and disadvantages. Determining these pros and cons can help a business to draw an action plan to overcome the challenges and hurdles that may come up along the way.

Advantages of Online Collaboration

1. Convenience in Organizing Meetings

One of the key advantages of online collaboration is that it makes it easier for people who aren't in the same location to work together. Most companies have branches and/or offices in multiple cities and countries. And to ensure those working on a given project are informed and engaged, the use of online collaboration software is important. For instance, ezTalks Cloud Meeting can allow up to 500 participants to join in a meeting and listen to the presenter at once. With such a huge meeting capacity, company employees can effectively call for a meeting and collaborate with one another, regardless of their geographical differences.

2. Easier Management of Projects

With the ability to convene a meeting at anytime from anywhere, online collaboration makes it easier to manage team projects. For instance, when introducing or analyzing a new company product, the production team may need to work with other departments like Research & Development (RD), marketing and sales. Online collaboration software provides an ideal platform for all these players to engage in meaningful discussions about the proposed product. That means the person in charge of the product department can generate a report quite seamlessly and submit it to the bosses within the set timelines.

3. Faster Completion of Projects

When different stakeholders are involved in a given project, each of them is likely to give the best input in terms of expertise. A collaborative team that recognizes its synergies can have excellent viable solutions shared quickly and decisions reached in time. Once the conclusions have been tabled, presented to the bosses and approved, the next phase will obviously be implementation. Online collaboration can particularly fuel faster completion of projects since project stakeholders can meet and interact online without experiencing time constraints and inconveniences.

4. Significant Cost Savings

If those participating in a meeting are many, it can sometimes be a challenge to find a physical space that can accommodate everyone. Online collaboration software allows businesses to host online meetings in real time with hundreds of participants interacting simultaneously. Employees can actually call for urgent meetings and discuss important project issues using the minimal resources. It doesn't really matter whether one is at home, on the road or in the office. EzTalks Cloud Meeting provides users with innovative whiteboards and screen sharing options that make collaborative sessions even more engaging. The use of telepresence video conferencing particularly simulates the real-life meeting rooms, which makes mastering facial expressions and body language easy. With such robust online collaboration solutions, there's no need to book flights, hotel rooms or meeting spaces. Online meetings can simply be organized and disseminated instantly over a virtual meeting room. In the long run, a business utilizing online collaboration will experience improved performance and productivity while enjoying significant cost savings on communication.

Disadvantages of Online Collaboration

1. Lack of Face-To-Face Interaction

While online collaboration through video conferencing provides real-time communication between people, it lacks the aspect of face-to-face interaction. For instance, meeting participants cannot argue with one another simultaneously over the online platform because of longer lag times. That may sometimes limit the level of engagement of the employees in an online meeting. And when the quality of video stream is poor, it's difficult for meeting attendees to decipher facial expressions and body language of the presenter.

2. Possibility of Network Failure and Equipment Breakdown

Online collaboration might provide a range convenient and efficient meeting options but network failure and equipment breakdown might limit its use. Participating in online collaboration meetings through video conference also requires the use of huge data bundles, which can be limiting to some attendees. Running out of data bundles leads to disconnection from the internet, which bars attendees from participating in collaborative efforts of finding solutions to a project. Meeting interruptions due to any of these reasons may cause a cross-collaboration team to work beyond the scheduled timelines in order to complete the project. That can delay project discussions and subsequently decision making, which might have significant cost implications.

3. Language and Cultural Differences

The use of online collaboration software has made it easier for companies to bring together employees from different countries to collaborate in a given project. While that might be a good strategy to improve performance, differences in language and culture can limit the engagement of employees working in different regions. That means online collaboration cannot offer meaningful solutions in this case.

4. Incidences of Group Think

Bringing stakeholders from different departments and region to work together may undoubtedly inspire fresh perspectives on the project. However, there is always the threat of group think, where stronger personalities may take over the discussions, persuade and supplant the ideas of others. Such online collaborations might lead to the bosses believing the outcome is a group effort yet it's something that was agreed upon by a few. That might end up lowering the performance of a project as important ideas may be left out in the process.

Conclusion

While the benefits of online collaboration are many, there are potential drawbacks that come along too. That does not mean companies should avoid adopting the online collaboration software. Rather, they should seek to understand how applicable the software is to the business. The effective use of online collaborations basically depends on how the business analyses the problems and the strategies it puts in place to eradicate them. By adopting online collaboration software, a business can take advantage of convenient hosting of meetings, swift project management and improved savings on communication. But in order to keep the system working, the business should focus on fixing the issues of quality video streaming, internet/software breakdown and language and cultural barriers. This is all any size of business needs to do.

What is internet for ecommerce function

What are advantages of online shopping? Due to rapid growth of technology, business organizations have switched over from the traditional method of selling goods to electronic method of selling goods. Business organizations use internet as a main vehicle to conduct commercial transact . Its advantages include: Online stores do not have space constraints and a wide variety of products can be displayed on websites. It helps the analytical buyers to purchase a product after a good search. Convenience of online shopping, it means that customers can purchase items from the comfort of their own homes or work place. Shopping is made easier and convenient for the customer through internet. It is also easy to cancel the transactions.

The following table depicts the factors which motivate the online shoppers to buy products online.

Top 6 reasons given by shoppers in buying through internet

- Saves time and efforts.
- Convenience of Shopping at home.
- Wide variety / range of products are available.
- Good discounts / lower prices.
- Get detailed information of the product.
- We can compare various models / brands.

2. No pressure shopping

Generally, in physical stores, the sales representatives try to influence the buyers to buy the product. There can be some kind of pressure, whereas the customers are not pressurized in any way in online stores.

3. Online shopping saves time

Customers do not have to stand in queues in cash counters to pay for the products that have been purchased by them. They can shop from their home or work place and do not have to spend time traveling. The customers can also look for the products that are required by them by entering the key words or using search engines.

4. Comparisons

Companies display the whole range of products offered by them to attract customers with different tastes and needs. This enables the buyers to choose from a variety of models after comparing the finish, features and price of the products on display, Sometimes, price comparisons are also available online.

5. Availability of online shop

The mall is open on 365 x 24 x 7. So, time does not act as a barrier, wherever the vendor and buyers are.

6. Online tracking

Online consumers can track the order status and delivery status tracking of shipping is also available.

7. Online shopping saves money

To attract customers to shop online, e-tailers and marketers offer discounts to the customers. Due to elimination of maintenance, real-estate cost, the retailers are able to sell the products with attractive discounts through online. Sometimes, large online shopping sites offer store comparison.

Disadvantages of online shopping

Ease of use is the prime reason that drives the success of e-commerce. Though internet provides a quick and easy way to purchase a product, some people prefer to use this technology only in a limited way. They regard internet as a means for gathering more information about a product before buying it in a shop. Some people also fear that they might get addicted to online shopping.

The major disadvantages of online shopping are as follows.

1. Delay in delivery

Long duration and lack of proper inventory management result in delays in shipment. Though the duration of selecting, buying and paying for an online product may not take more than 15 minutes; the delivery of the product to customer' s doorstep takes about 1-3 weeks. This frustrates the customer and prevents them from shopping online.

2. Lack of significant discounts in online shops

Physical stores offer discounts to customers and attract them so this makes it difficult for e-tailors to compete with the offline platforms.

3. Lack of touch and feel of merchandise in online shopping

Lack of touch-feel-try creates concerns over the quality of the product on offer. Online shopping is not quite suitable for clothes as the customers cannot try them on.

4. Lack of interactivity in online shopping

Physical stores allow price negotiations between buyers and the seller. The show room sales attendant representatives provide personal attention to customers and help them in purchasing goods. Certain online shopping mart offers service to talk to a sales representative,

5. Lack of shopping experience

The traditional shopping exercise provides lot of fun in the form of show-room atmosphere, smart sales attendants, scent and sounds that cannot be experienced through a website. Indians generally enjoy shopping. Consumers look forward to it as an opportunity to go out and shop.

6. Lack of close examination in online shopping

A customer has to buy a product without seeing actually how it looks like. Customers may click and buy some product that is not really required by them. The electronic images of a product are sometimes misleading. The color, appearance in real may not match with the electronic images. People like to visit physical stores and prefer to have close examination of good, though it consumes time.

The electronic images vary from physical appearance when people buy goods based on electronic images.

7. Frauds in online shopping

Sometimes, there is disappearance of shopping site itself. In addition to above, the online payments are not much secured. So, it is essential for e-marketers and retailers to pay attention to this issue to boost the growth of e-commerce. The rate of cyber crimes has been increasing and customers' credit card details and bank details have been misused which raise privacy issues. Customers have to be careful in revealing their personal information. Some of the e-tailors are unreliable.

The disadvantages of online shopping will not hinder its growth, Online shopping helped businesses to recover from the recession. Merchants should pay attention to the stumbling blocks and ensure secure payment system to make online shopping effective, The following advice may be followed by the E-merchants and by the online shoppers.

Advantages and Disadvantages of Ecommerce

E-commerce, or the act of selling goods or services online as opposed to selling at brick and mortar establishments, has reshaped the modern marketplace in recent years, but this new form of trade comes with its own sets of advantages and disadvantages over traditional methods. It's important, then, for businesses to look beyond the hype and develop their own perspectives on the true value of e-commerce—to business and to consumers—because interestingly, there are many advantages for consumers that might actually be a disadvantage for e-commerce businesses. Among the top advantages for starting an e-commerce business are eliminating geographical limitations, gaining new customers with search engine visibility, lower costs for maintenance and rent, and higher capacity for goods and deliveries while the core disadvantages of starting an e-commerce business include losing the personal touch of physical retailers, delaying goods or services deliveries, and limiting availability of merchandise as some goods cannot be sold online. Explore the following article to discover whether or not venturing

into e-commerce is right for your business.
Advantages to Physical Retailers

The Internet might be the single most important facet of modern society, governing everything from political discourse and higher education to the way we conduct ourselves and our businesses. It's no wonder, then, that switching your business to an e-commerce model would come with a huge amount of advantages.
On top of eliminating the need for long lines at physical stores, e-commerce sites allow people who are not situated in major urban areas access to stores located remotely. E-commerce, as a result, opens new markets for your business, allowing you to develop a new business model geared toward your expanding consumer base, especially one that relies on good e-commerce Search Engine Optimization to drive more free traffic to the site through consumers' use of search engines.
Since you also eliminate the need for a physical store, your business can save money on rent and upkeep like utilities and maintenance. Additionally, because there is no limit to the number of items that can be sold online, your store's stock can expand exponentially by moving to an e-commerce model, and the store can remain open 24/7 so consumers can browse your wares at their leisure.
The most important advantages to e-commerce, consumers can also purchase digital goods like music albums, videos, or books instantaneously, and stores can now sell unlimited copies of these digital items. This also cuts down on things like employee payroll expenses because you no longer need to have dozens of employees a week on-site to sell albums, books, or movies. E-commerce also allows your business to scale up easier than physical retailers as they are not bound by physical limitations like inventory storage space. Of course, logistics gets tougher as a business grows, but one can scale up its logistics, too, with the choice of the right third-party logistics provider. Since the e-commerce merchant captures contact information in the form of email, sending out automated and customized emails is quite easy. Additionally, these businesses

and metrics allow for superior store customization by using cookies and other methods of monitoring a consumer's behavior, because the entire supply chain can be interlinked with business to business e-commerce systems, procurement becomes faster, transparent, and cheaper, and there's no need to handle currency notes or cash, which further cuts down on costs and opportunities for accounting errors.

Finally, e-commerce allows your business to track logistics, which is key to a successful e-commerce company, as well as sell low-volume goods. Although conventional retail focuses on stocking fast-moving goods, the economics of e-commerce permits slow-moving and even obsolete products to be included in the catalog.

While it may appear that e-commerce is the perfect choice to solve your business problems, there are still a number of disadvantages to switching from selling at a physical location to using online retail. Many consumers still prefer visiting brick and mortar shops because of their personal touch and the relationship customers get to develop with a retail location. Additionally, many customers want to experience the product before purchase, especially when it comes to clothing, but e-commerce eliminates that luxury.

Security and credit card fraud are also huge risks when dealing with online shopping—consumers run the risk of identity fraud and other hazards as their personal details are captured by e-commerce businesses while businesses run the risk of phishing attacks and other forms of security fraud; both can suffer from credit card fraud. As a result, consumers also fear their inability to identify scams and scammers, meaning that your website has to be extraordinarily protected and verified for most consumers to trust using it.

If shopping is about instant gratification, then consumers are left empty-handed for some time after making a purchase on an e-commerce website as they often have to either pay more for expedited shipping or wait out several days while the postal service does its job. Additionally, if they are unsatisfied with their order, many e-commerce retailers have to issue a refund, which requires your business to expand its reverse logistics functions, meaning the shipping back of goods and refunding of costs.

Speaking of costs, there's a multiplicity of regulations and taxation that comes with opening an e-commerce shop, and regulators are still not clear about the tax implications of e-commerce transactions, which is especially true when the seller and buyer are located in different territories.

What ecommerce benefits to consumers and weaknesses to ecommerce businessmen? Some concerns don't necessarily fit in just the pro's or con's side of the argument—these unique issues present an advantage to shoppers and consumers while increasing difficulty for businesses, meaning that while more customers might be coming to the shop, the business is suffering in another way. While it's easier for consumers to compare prices because of several shopping search engines and websites, sellers might find it too restrictive to their business revenues as many get filtered out of the consumer's consideration set. Though there is nothing about e-commerce that makes it intrinsically oriented to discounts, the way online business has evolved has led to lowered prices online, which acts as an advantage for the buyer, but a disadvantage for the seller. The consumer experiences the convenience of having goods home-delivered, but the logistics involved with delivering each individual item adds substantial strain to the e-commerce business operation, making it great for profits and customer retention but terrible for logistics and management.

There are several businesses in the marketplace that trade solely online. In setting up an online business, the owner will need to go through the same procedures as a traditional business, in formulating a business plan, by crafting a mission statement and through handling other administrative matters. However, there are a number of advantages and disadvantages of operating an online business, points worth considering as you prepare to launch your enterprise.

Reduced Costs

The main advantage of having an online business is the cost

difference when compared to setting up a traditional office-based company. While there are fees associated with securing a domain and setting up a website, these are minimal in comparison to leasing and maintaining physical premises.

Reduced Staff Requirements

Whereas in a physical retail outlet the owner would need to recruit a number of sales staff, with an online business a lot of the work is carried out automatically. For example, purchasing an item online does not require a cashier to take payment: a purchaser simply enters his or her card details and the item is paid for within minutes.

Wider Range

With an online business is that you can market your company on a global scale, reaching potential customers in other countries and continents. You will need to have systems in place in order to dispatch your goods or services to these far-away locations, however. Nevertheless, whereas a physical business can only advertise to customers in a local area, having an online business means you can expose your company to a large number of potential customers.

Saturated Marketplace

Having an online presence does, however, mean that you are surrounded by other businesses within your industry, all desperate to expose their company to a wide audience. As a result, your business may become lost in a sea of similar companies, in which case you will need to discover a product or element to your firm that gives you an edge over your competitors.

Lack of Interaction

With a physical presence staff members can interact with customers face to face. This can impress the purchaser and prompt them to share their positive experiences with others. Some purchasers may simply prefer face-to-face interaction, as opposed to purchasing their goods online. You may struggle to develop a meaningful relationship with a purchaser when you operate an online business.

Support Systems

If a customer purchases an item from a physical store, only to later discover it is faulty, they can return the product to the store for an exchange or refund by means of a relatively easy process. However, if an online purchaser finds that their goods are faulty, it could be several days until the issue is rectified, especially if you have no customer care system in operation. You will need to implement a structured policy and system for refunding faulty goods to avoid customer frustration.

Internet Connectivity

You could stand to lose a lot of time and money if, for some reason, your website goes down and cannot be fixed for hours, or even days. This could cause potential customers to be dissuaded from buying a product from you if they receive an error message when trying to visit your website, and they may communicate their poor experience with friends and family.

Will e-commerce replace traditional retail business in India? Why?

Will Books get out of fashion because there is a Kindle nowadays? Will Netflix (or Amazon Prime) replace Cinema Halls? What do you think? Or will you completely stop going to office because there is something called virtual meeting? All of this is happening, and someday sooner than we believe they will overtake the human interaction required to achieve the same output. Yes, the human emotions would die that day!

There is no easy answer to this question, especially when we are at a juncture where things are changing at a rapid pace in everything which has a digital version attached to it. Considering that human society is designed in a way which requires people to stay together and co-operate in order to get through a day, all the things which we come across in our daily lives requires a human interaction to be considered completed. Earlier we had no option but to meet face to face and get things done, but then we got unique technology tools & devices which could eliminate the need for our physical presence and replace that human identity and authenticity by establishing the trust technologically. Phones have long replaced the effort required for me to visit a LPG dealer and place an order. Or when my washing machine fails, I do not think twice before placing a service request and I am completely convinced that some human being sitting on the other side of the phone will make sure to send someone to repair my washing machine.

Can e-commerce bring benefits to India businessmen? They feel that they don't need to waste their time. Their Phone will reach where I will be located three days from now. Human life is always about customization. And it is customization which needs a human touch and a face to face interaction. Will technology ever be able to fill this gap? Certainly. And if not technology, such gaps will be filled by smart businessmen. Slowly and Steadily, all the commerce will be done over the wire (or wireless), and all that needs is a smart businessman to make it real.

Advantages and disadvantages of online retailing

Online retailing is growing at an astonishing rate, with online sales now accounting for around one quarter of the total retail market. Retailers who ignore e-commerce may see their trade lessening as customers continue to shift to ordering products online. However you need to think carefully and weigh all the advantages and disadvantages - backed by good market research - before deciding on whether or not to trade online.

Advantages of online retail

The benefits of retailing online include:

● Easy access to market - in many ways the access to market for entrepreneurs has never been easier. Online marketplaces such as eBay and Amazon allow anyone to set up a simple online shop and sell products within minutes. See ● selling through online marketplaces.

● Reduced overheads - selling online can remove the need for expensive retail premises and customer-facing staff, allowing you to invest in better marketing and customer experience on your e-commerce site.

● Potential for rapid growth - selling on the internet means traditional constraints to retail growth - eg finding and paying for larger - are not major factors. With a good digital marketing strategy and a plan a scale up order fulfilment systems, you can respond and boost growing sales. See ● planning for e-commerce.

● Widen your market / export - one major advantage over premises-based retailers is the ability expand your market beyond local customers very quickly. You may discover a strong demand for your products in other countries which you can respond to by targeted marketing, offering your website in a different language, or perhaps partnering with an overseas company. See ● basics of exporting.

● Customer intelligence - ability to use online marketing tools to target new customers and website analysis tools to gain insight into your customers' needs. For advice on improving your customer's on-site experience see ● measuring your online marketing.

Disadvantages of online retail

Some negatives of online retail include:

● Website costs - planning, designing, creating, hosting, securing and maintaining a professional e-commerce website isn't cheap, especially if you expect large and growing sales volumes. See ● common e-commerce pitfalls.

● Infrastructure costs - even if you aren't paying the cost of customer-facing premises, you'll need to think about the costs of physical space for order fulfilment, warehousing goods, dealing with returns and staffing for these tasks. See ● fulfilling online orders.

● Security and fraud - the growth of online retail market has attracted the attention of sophisticated criminal elements. The reputation of your business could be fatally damaged if you don't invest in the latest security systems to protect your website and transaction processes. See ● e-commerce pitfalls - security weaknesses.

● Legal issues - getting to grips with e-commerce and the law can be a challenge and you'll need to be aware of, and plan to cope with, the additional customer rights which are attached to online sales.

See ● the law and selling online.

● Advertising costs - while online marketing can be a very efficient way of getting the right customers to your products, it demands a generous budget. This is especially true if you are competing in a crowded sector or for popular keywords. See ● pay-per-click and paid search advertising.

● Customer trust - it can be difficult to establish a trusted brand name, especially without a physical business with a track record and face-to-face interaction between customers and sales staff. You need to consider the costs or setting up a good customer service system as part of your online offering. See ● manage your customer service.

E-commerce offers many ways retailers can reach consumers and conduct business without the need for a brick-and-mortar storefront. Today, it's almost economic suicide for any retailer not to be able to sell online. However, before you enter the world of e-commerce, be familiar with the advantages and disadvantages of selling online.

Advantages of E-Commerce

retailers can increase their sales and profits faster than a brick and mortar establishment because selling online offers the advantage of being open twenty-four hours a day, seven days a week. Selling online also allows retailers to sell their merchandise in any part of the world without additional expense. This means e-retailers can expand into global markets or target an extremely focused segment, such as selling burkas to Middle Eastern women. While the small retail store on Main Street would never dream of competing with a national chain retailer, a mom-and-pop shop may find itself on a more level playing field with its big-box competitors.

People can find your brand and interact with it when you establish an online presence, including tapping into a whole new (potential) customer base. Much of online traffic is organic, meaning that if you build your e-store correctly, customers will find you without spending a dime. All you need is a robust Facebook, Twitter, or other social media platform to spread the news. Also, while traditional advertising is very costly, if you do get involved in digital advertising, the cost is nominal.

Disadvantages of Selling Online

One of the biggest disadvantages of selling online is the continued battle with security. Shoppers are becoming more relaxed with providing their personal and credit card information, but security concerns are still keeping many consumers from shopping online. Retailers selling online exclusively may have to work harder to build trust and establish a relationship with their customers. Personal interaction is limited when online selling and there is plenty of competition in cyberspace. Store owners may find it very difficult to find repeat customers. As online retailers expand their customer base to include shoppers in other countries, they also increase the difficulties in delivering their goods. The retailer is responsible for all deliverables and if the customer does not receive their products immediately, it is ultimately the retailer's responsibility to resolve the issue.

Online Banking - Advantages and Disadvantages

The World Wide Web has permeated virtually every aspect of modern life. If you have access to a computer with an Internet connection, an almost limitless amount of goods, services and entertainment choices are at your fingertips. You can do just about anything online, including your banking and financial transactions. But is this wise? Just how comfortable are you conducting your banking business in cyberspace? After all, online banking has both advantages and disadvantages, namely:

Advantages

- It's generally secure. But make sure that the website you're using has a valid security certificate. This let's you know that the site is protected from cyber-thieves looking to steal your personal and financial information.
- You have twenty-four-hour access. When your neighborhood
- bank closes, you can still access your account and make transactions online. It's a very convenient alternative for those that can't get to the bank during normal hours because of their work

schedule, health or any other reason.

● You can access your account from virtually anywhere. If you're on a business trip or vacationing away from home, you can still keep a watchful on your money and financial transactions - regardless of your location.

● Conducting business online is generally faster than going to the bank. Long teller lines can be time-consuming, especially on a Pay Day. But online, there are no lines to contend with. You can access your account instantly and at your leisure.

● Many features and services are typically available online. For example, with just a few clicks you can apply for ● loans, check the progress of your ● investments, review ● interest rates and gather other important information that may be spread out over several different brochures in the local bank.

Disadvantages

● Yes, online banking is generally secure, but it certainly isn't always secure. ● Identity theft is running rampant, and banks are by no means immune. And once your information is compromised, it can take months or even years to correct the damage, not to mention possibly costing you thousands of dollars, as well.

● Some online banks are more stable than others. Not all online setups are an extension of a brick-and-mortar bank. Some operate completely in cyberspace, without the benefit of an branch that you can actually visit if need be. With no way to physically check out the operation, you must be sure to thoroughly do your homework about the bank's background before giving them any of your money.

● Before using a banking site that you aren't familiar with, check to make sure that their deposits are-insured. If not, you could possibly lose all of your deposits if the bank goes under, or its major shareholders decide to take an extended vacation in Switzerland.

● Customer service can be below the quality that you're used to. Some people simply take comfort in being able to talk to another human being face-to-face if they experience a problem. Although most major banks employ a dedicated customer service department specifically for online users, going through the dreaded telephone menu can still be quite irritating to many. Again, some are considerably better (or worse) than others.

● Not all online transactions are immediate. Online banking is subject to the same business-day parameters as traditional banking. Therefore, printing out and keeping receipts is still very important, even when banking online.

Online banking does have pros and cons. However, it's not only the wave of the future, it's the wave right now, and the clock isn't likely to go backward. If you take reasonable care to safeguard your personal and financial information, you'll likely find that online banking is a convenient tool that you can easily live with. Eventually, you'll probably even wonder how you ever lived without it.

With increasing the need of eCommerce industry, every businessman is looking to have an online store where they can sell their range of products and services. One can get a lot of benefits by opting for eCommerce as it delivers a comprehensive range of benefits to retailers and merchants

Electronic Commerce is also known as e-commerce that consists of the purchasing and selling of products or services through electronic systems like computer networks and the Internet. In this modern world of technology, e-commerce is becoming a very significant option for many businesses as there are lots of companies that are interested in developing their online stores.

With increasing demand for online purchasing, more and more businesses are moving to e-store from brick and mortar stores. In the US, more than 60% of people are purchasing goods online from the comfort of their home and this figure is increasing constantly. By considering this percentage, we can say that e-commerce is expanding tremendously because of its complete range of benefits that any industry vertical can enjoy. Today, e-Commerce has revolutionized the way companies are doing business. Now, consumers can purchase almost anything online 24*7 a day and get an ultimate shopping experience. Before you opt for an e-

Commerce business, have a look on its comprehensive benefits that you can enjoy:

Convenience & Easiness:

For many people in the world, e-Commerce becomes one of the preferred ways of shopping as they enjoy their online because of its easiness and convenience. They are allowed to buy products or services from their home at any time of day or night The best thing about it is buying options that are quick, convenient and user-friendly with the ability to transfer funds online. Because of its convenience, consumers can save their lots of time as well as money by searching their products easily and making purchasing online.

Offer Product Datasheets:

Consumers can also get description and details from an online product catalog. For your customers, it is very much important to get information about the product no matter whether the time of day and day of the week. Through information, your customers and prospects are making decision to purchase your products or not.

Attract New Customers with Search Engine Visibility:

As we all know that physical retail is run by branding and relationships. But, online retail is also driving by traffic that comes from search engines. For customers, it is not very so common to follow a link in the search engine results and land up on an ecommerce website that they never heard of.

Comprise Warranty Information:

No matter whether you are looking to choose including warranty information with product descriptions and datasheets or providing it from within an ecommerce shopping cart, you need to make sure that customers must be aware of important terms and conditions that are associated with their purchase.

Decreasing cost of inventory Management:

With e-commerce business, the suppliers can decrease the cost of managing their inventory of goods that they can automate the inventory management using web-based management system. Indirectly, they can save their operational costs.

Keep Eye on Consumers' Buying Habit:

The best thing is e-commerce retailers can easily keep a constant eye on consumers' buying habits and interests to tailors their offer suit to consumers' requirements. By satisfying their needs constantly, you can improve your ongoing relationship with them and build long-lasting relationships.

Competence:

For effective business transactions, e-commerce is an efficient and competence method. Setting-up cost is extremely low as compare to expanding your business with more brick and mortar locations. Very few licenses and permits are required to start-up an online business than physical store. You can save your lots of money by using fewer employees to perform operations like billing customers, managing inventory and more.

Allow Happy Customers to Sell Your Products:

With lots of customers' reviews and product ratings, you can easily increase your sells as new customers find that your products are good and effective. Make sure that you mention your clients' testimonials, reviews and product ratings as such things can help your new customers to purchase your products.

Selling Products Across the World:

If you are running a physical store, it will be limited by the geographical area that you can service, but with an e-Commerce website, you can sell your products and services across the world. The entire world is your playground, where you can sell your complete range of products without any geographical limits. Moreover, the remaining limitation of geography has dissolved by commerce that is also known as mobile commerce.

Stay open 24*7/365 days:

One of the most important benefits that ecommerce merchants can enjoy is store timings are now 24/7/365 as they can run e-commerce websites all the time. By this way, they can increase their sales by boosting their number of orders. However, it is also beneficial for customers as they can purchase products whenever they want no matter whether it is early morning or mid-night.

Economy:

Now, you don't have to invest your money in the physical store, insurance or infrastructure as all you need is a wonderful idea, unique products and well-designed website to reach your precious customers to sell your products and services. We can say that this makes an e-commerce a lot more economical and reasonable.

Boost Brand Awareness:

As like e-commerce business can help B2B organizations to get new customers, so it will be helpful for e-commerce businesses to boost their brand awareness in the market. Developing pages that can be indexed by search engines crawlers is one of the best ways to enhance your website' search engine optimization and enhance the target audience on your site.

Decrease Costs:

One of the most positive things about eCommerce is that you can decrease the costs of your business. Below are some of the costs that you can reduce by opting for ecommerce:

● Advertising & Marketing Cost: If you opt for ecommerce, you don't have to spend your money on advertising and marketing. However, organic search engine traffic, social media traffic and pay-per-click are some of the advertising channels that are cost-effective.

● Personnel: A complete automation of check-out, billing, inventory management, payments and other type of operational costs lower the total number of employees that you require to run your ecommerce business.

● Eliminate Travel Cost: Now, customers do not have to travel long distances to reach their desired stores as ecommerce allows them to visit the e-store anytime without traveling. With few mouse clicks, customers can make their purchase and have wonderful shopping experience.

Offer Huge Information:

One of the best benefits of ecommerce for customers is they can get huge information that is not possible in a physical store. We all know that it is quite difficult to equip employees to respond to customers who are looking for information on different product lines.

But ecommerce websites offer additional information to their customers without any hassle. All the given information is provided by vendors so that their customers find it easy to purchase products with information.

Analytics:

We can say that business 2 business offers an excellent platform to organizations to launch their complete range of analytics campaign. Through ecommerce, organizations can easily calculate and evaluate sales effectiveness, customer effectiveness, marketing campaigns, product mix, customer engagement and more.

Expand Market for Niche Products:

It is difficult for buyers and sellers to find each other in the physical world, but it becomes very easy for them with the inception of e-store. Customers can search their required products on the web and can purchase it from any corner of the world. No matter what kind of product customers are looking, they can find all types of products without any hassle.

Scalability:

With effective ecommerce solution, you and your organization grow and scale easily to meet market demand as well as customer requirements by introducing different sales channels and reaching market segments.

Ability of Multi-site:

With ecommerce platform, it becomes easy for businesses to launch channel specific and particular brand ecommerce website. This ability enables you to provide co-branded websites for your specific customers and allows for websites catering to specific international spectators.

IN conclusion, future internet remote working mode and online business will be more popular and it can be easier accepted to be used by working people and businessmen in our society , due to they can bring time saving and cost saving functions to them.

CHAPTER FOUR

Computer technology related service consumer negative emotion

Technology negative influence reasons

- 1.1 Online technology negative influence

Nowadays , internet is a popular tool to be provided to human to apply, e.g. online commerce brings businessmen to do online business trading, online searching information brings anyone can find information in short time, online studying can brings online learning chance and none classroom attendance to students. However, if we often do any online behavior, it will influence our mental and physical health to be poor, e.g. often spending time to use internet for social media contact. This interactive technologies will influence every young people's brain, behavior and attitude to be poor because they often spend time to use computer at home. Then, this digital technologies will lead them to lack nervous to study or learn any new knowledge, when who are students if they often apply computer to learn and they do not need to contact classmates and teachers in classrooms. Consequently, their school examination results will be possible influenced to be bad if they often apply computer to learn because they do not spend other time to any recreational activities or contacting people to make friends activities in their daily life.

It brings these two questions:
(1) Will internet often be used use to influence young people's mental and physical health to be poor?
(2) Has it bring direct negative impact relationship when young people often spend time to use interest to do learning and information research behavior to cause poor mental and physical health?
Nowadays, human often uses internet which is one part of our habit. Our lives have become increasingly abuse in technology. Much of our communication and research is now online, much of our leisure and entertainment is provided by the internet and video games , and many of use internet find our mobile phones have become one essential part of our connectivity and everyday organizes to control our normal behaviors and to influence my normal life style poorly.
With these changes in lifestyle questions are it will arise negative influence about what technology may bring negative influence to us. Some of these questions bring potential detrimental effects, which had being unpredicted crisis in which the human brain is under threat from the modern world. Considerately, it influences the teenagers learning behaviors and attitudes to be poor. It seems that they have possible cause negative impact effect relationship between internet abuse habit behavior and poor mental and physical health as well as poor learning attitude and poor learning behaviors to young students.
The main factor of often doing internet playing behavior will have disadvantages to young people, because they will apply the internet tools to play video games to enjoy greater attention. This reflects a special case of environmental factor influence on whose mind and brain and health to be poor. Otherwise, if young people only spend some time to apply internet tools to do any reasonable need and meaning behavior, e.g. searching jobs from internet or searching any university written articles for study reference for learning intention or working seeking intention. Then, internet is a good tool to help them to develop their further career . Even, internet will

train their brain and mind is more clear and clever and health to get advantages during who do any searching behavior for studying or learning intention from internet channel.

In conclusion, internet communication technology will bring either positive or negative influence to any users, it is depended on the user how to spend whose time to do any researching data or studying behavior in their daily time spending arrangement . Such as often playing game behavior or watching movie behavior and listening music entertainment behavior , which will have negative influence to any internet users' mind and physical health to be poor. Otherwise, sometimes searching jobs or seeking teaching articles or newspapers to read for learning intention from internet tool, which will have positive influence to any internet users. Hence, internet technology must not bring negative influence to human, it can also bring positive influence to human. It is depended on how we spend time to apply this high technology communication tools to do the beneficial mind and learning training behavior from this technological communication tool.

● How technology could contribute to bring poor standard of living to influence our societies

The effects of technology will have possible to bring global poor standard of living challenges. On the positive influence, especially science-based technology has offered a better world through the elimination of disease and material improvements to standards of living. But, on the negative influence, it will cause resource extraction, dangerous materials and pollution of air, water and oil have created conditions for unprecedented environmental to cause damage to the biosphere, when human applies any technologic tools to damage our earth natural environment in order to gain any profit for business aims.

Although technology brings businessmen to earn more profit, when who apply high technology to raise productivity and performance and efficiency to workers, e.g. artificial intelligence manufacturing robots, or they apply internet to sell their products (ecommerce),

but technology also brings these disadvantages: Despite the ongoing technological revolution, the majority of the world population still lives in poverty with inadequate food, poor housing and less energy supply, illness increase , due to technological manufacturing can influence clean water and fresh air to be polluted to influence human's bodies to be un-health. Specially, the populations in Africa, Asia development countries, illness and death ratio both is risen by water and air pollution in these development countries nowadays.
Thus, it seems that it has relationship to bring negative influence to us between technology and air/water pollution and rising illnesses and deaths. Also, human needs to consider technology will support and enhance productivity and performance and efficiency , but it also influence human quality of standard to be poor challenge as the same time occurrence.
However, I suggest that businessmen ought reduce to invest much productivity by technological manufacturing improvement method, who ought concern environment pollution challenges how to avoid to apply technology to bring negative influence to all human's poor health challenge for long time. If human can apply technology, such as positive tool to solve problems or knowledge of how to create things, such as to brew beer , good taste soft drink or fruit or to make an atomic bomb, and culture (or understanding of the world, our value-systems), e.g. agriculture , irrigation and clean water management and navigation technological skill improvement. It means knowledge, technology becomes understanding of how to make and use tools and instruments becomes encodes as technological knowledge and know-how.
Consequently, human's positive and responsible behavior will change technology tools to develop of modern scientific knowledge, based on observations, hypotheses and generalizations on the natural laws concerning the behavior of materials and the living environment.

How to avoid to technology brings
negative influence on children

● Technology negative influence to children

In this world, it becomes impossible to escape the constant connection with others, aside from completely dis-connective from it, and into the unknown. Thus, parents need to know how their children using technological tools of behavior, which will influence impact on their children positively or negatively.

Nowadays, laptops and smartphones are now in the hands of children or young as ten age, and the eight to eighteen age young people that this group spends on average of ten hours and forty-five minutes or day exposed to media.

Whether their high amount of contact electronic media behavior is a good thing or not. So what is the right answer? Which side has the correct insight? When we may not have the immediate answer, one must look into both sides of the argument and determine what the correct path for today's children is. Thus, it brings thing effect, such as: one decision is about technology use will affect today's children as they develop.

Whether technology in classroom is truly a benefit for students. The benefits include it can enrich basic skills. Students who have access to technology become more quickly in the material and , such as are able to absorb the information more quickly. Electronic material can be more stimulating and interactive for children, it is motivational since it provides ease to students in study conducted of advanced learning technology students have found to have more interested to attempt to do writing behavior.

Nowadays, children can use technology as a supplement with traditional education, but it is as not replacement. In fact, computers have been specifically useful, for they allow us to manipulate items, such as text to meet the needs of individual students. For example, text can be made larger so it can be seen easier and also read aloud for deaf students. Moreover, recently, specific devices have been engineers to cater to students with specific disabilities. Thus, it seems that the introduction of technology into modern culture has drastically shifted social norms to include technology into children's daily lives.

However, when technology had been applied essentially into children's daily live. Technology also had bad points. Today, it is not uncommon to bring children playing on their portable video game systems, when at a restaurant with their family or to see a child operating a computer better than some adults. If children were abuse to use computer to video game wherever they go to any places, such as restaurant, school, toilet, catching transportation tool to sit down to play video games by mobiles habitually. It will bring this social challenge: Can technology influence children choose not to pursue to spend much time to learn, instead of often spending time to play video games for entertainment aim by mobiles habitually.

Technology will part of word of the rest of our foreseeable lives. But if children often accustomed to apply technology tool to play any video games from mobiles and internet tool. Consequently, they will often devote nervous and time to spend to play any video games from mobiles conveniently any time. Just like there have to be rules of conduct in real life, there have not to be smart rule of conduct in digital life to children.

The pursue of this internet and video games entertainment technology will force or encourage children to the playing video games from internet skills to navigate it and keep up with it as they get old. Hence, to judge electronic media is beneficial or harmful to children's learning stage . It is depended on how the child chooses to apply computer and/or internet technology from electronic media tool. If the child often use internet and computer or mobile tool to go to anywhere to concentrate on playing video games. Then, I believe that it will bring harm to the child's future learning development. Otherwise, if the child often use internet and computer or mobile tool to learn or seek any education articles in classroom or library or at home, these electronic tools are as technology advances to learn media. Then , it will be beneficial to the child's future learning development.

Technology negative influence to low knowledge learner to feel difficult to adopt future new technological labor market

Nowadays, information technology development is rapid. It brings this question: Will it bring negative influence to low knowledge learner to feel difficult to adopt future new technological labor market, special in underdevelopment of culture countries' labor markets?

To answer this question, firstly, we need to know what the underdevelopment of culture countries' labor market means before to answer this question. Culture means adaptive behavior, has been an integral feature of the human species through its evolution, it is shared, learned, symbolic, and transmitted cross generationally. In another sense, culture refers to all non-biological aspects of human existence, including economics, politics and technology. Underdevelopment of culture countries' labor market means what labors are needed to the under knowledge or educational level countries' labor markets.

There are very strong beliefs that the adoption and usage of information technology has performed positive effects on the development of any country, but it is not present that it will can bring negative effects on the underdevelopment of the culture countries, e.g. Africa, island places' living people, these places are not reactive or are not reaching technology mature stage. So, it brings these questions:

- What if the rate of adoption exceeds society's or individual's ability to adapt, when the rapid introduction of information technology?
- What if economic benefits are distributed in ways that are socially destabilizing?
- What if income distribution is unfair, with higher skilled personal becoming better compensated, when many people are deskilled and effectively unemployed of jobs comparable to their current jobs and at salaries comparable to what they are earning today?
- Can their low knowledgeable workers feel difficult to learn any

high technological skill to prepare their future job demand in these underdevelopment countries?

It seems rapid information technology to underdevelopment culture countries , which have chances to cause social challenges. Such as low skilled workers' unemployment , even office workers' salaries or technology manufacturing factory workers' wages will be reduced if who would not adapt the new technology development to follow the new technology influence to impact their work culture or method.

Thus, it also seems that culture can't exist without some form of society, i.e. culture us social. Therefore, cultural factors are observed in the society as providing to the production of its members who need to apply technological tools to manufacture products or serve their clients in their job responsibilities, e.g. factory workers, restaurant waiters etc. low skilled and learned workers. They need to learn how to apply new technology to work, e.g. computer skill or artificial intelligent skill.

So, it explains why rapid technology development will influence the low culture under development countries' low knowledge and low skillful workers to feel difficult to adapt how to learn to apply new technology production in themselves countries' technological job nature development change . Then , it will cause social challenges, such as unemployment, reducing wages, dismiss them, raising domestic labor market competition.

Moreover, some scientists concerned with the negative labor competition impact effect of information technology on the underdevelopment countries' low knowledgeable level of workers rather than the economic contribution of IT, because when many low knowledgeable level of workers feel difficult to learn technological skill to do their jobs, then they will be dismissed possible to bring social unemployment number to be increased and shortage of labor in these underdevelopment culture countries . In essence, they was asking if IT would erode this unique possession , even if it seems to contribute to their economic development.

Consequently, the intensive use of computer by the low knowledgeable skillful labors before the realization of whose thought –high technological production method itself may prevent the low knowledgeable workers' productive form being able to develop as a creatively thinking personally. This is a negative example of a mental process to them, which has been defined earlier.

In conclusion, the development of a new information society to under development culture countries would then raise a number of fundamental problems, one of which could be how to formulate and create optional cognitive preconditions for successful low knowledgeable labor' upgrade of high technological skill in short term. There are some pf the problems faced by developing nations who are still to development their technological production skill to low knowledgeable workers to let them feel difficult properly, let alone creating optimal preconditions for a successful mental process of low knowledge labor-computer interaction. At present, the adoption of IT in developing counties needed to be concern how to adapt whose countries' information technological labor users' production skill change.

The negative impact of smartphones/ mobiles and desktop/ laptop on human health and life

● Avoidance to driving and speaking mobile at the same time

Nowadays, the smartphones being a very new invention of humanity, became an inherent part of human's life. The smartphone combines different features. It allows users to keep pictures, memories, personal information correspondence, health and financial data in one place. Smartphones also become an integral part of modern telecommunications facilities. In some regions of the world, they are the most reliable only
of available places. The phones allow people to maintain continuous communication without interruption of their movement and

distances. However, recent scientific facts and research analysis of the smartphones' usage has disadvantages to influence human health and life.

The main key points indicate the effect of electromagnetic waves on human brains, effect of handheld device usage on human's upper extremities, back and neck. A significant neglect influence between the total time spend using mobile device each day and pain in the right shoulder and between times spent internet browsing and pain at the base of the right thumb. Moreover, mass cellphone calls enhance risk to human safety, e.g. when they are driving and listening and talking to touch mobiles at the same time. The drivers' driving and phoning calls behavior at the same time which will be very dangerous of their speaking and driving to cause traffic accident occurrence in possible. Thus, drivers can not neglect to avoid to do the mobile speaking and driving behavior at the same time when they are driving to reduce their traffic accident occurrence to cause their death or hurt in possible.

- What are the negative effect of electromagnetic waves on human brains from smartphone influence

Scientists proved that the smartphone is a source of the eminence of electromagnetic waves. Numerous studies have been conducted in the past years to identify the effect of electromagnetic waves emitted from the cell phones on human health.

However, it has not proved smartphone can influence our health certainly. As soon as mobile phones more and more part of our lives, the world is continuing research to prove whether cell phones are harmful to human health.

Today, there is no official statement announced by laboratory or medical center to answer this question: The complexity of the analysis of the statistical data makes the task more difficult for researchers. The impact of harmful radiation emitted from cell phones is still being studies.

Nowadays, human are accepted to use mobile phone in any time, any where popularly. Although, mobile is a good small size and convenient carrying of communication tool for human to use when we need to make phone calls to anyone in anywhere and any time conveniently. But, I feel that it will harm human health when we often use this communication tool any time.

However, some doctors indicate cell phones can cause brain cancer risk easily. But they have not any evidences to prove it is truth nowadays. Hence, the statement that cell phones can cause cancer has been not confirmed. The studies failed to prove that cellphones make a major risk develop cancer among frequent users. The main issues when conducting studies are some people may not accurately report the usage as they don't exactly remember how often they use the cell phone excluding speaker phone , and it is still difficult to measure the impact of other factors that may accelerate the cancer development for excessive cell phone users.

Although, it is not proved that cellphone can use brain cancer to human when we often use. But some scientists or medical professionals have proved that the cell phone users often use cell phones , it is possible to cause human physical illnesses, such as upper extremities, back and neck caused unhealthy and pain.

A smartphone or handhelds device combines advanced computing capability, such as internet communication, information retrieval, video, e-commerce and other features, that make device highly popular among people. According to Pew research center investigating, it showed that the number of smartphone owners comprises 56% of American adults in 2013 year and their average daily use of the device is about 195 minutes. The number of cellphone users increase every year. Various studies show the connection between cellphones usage and physical illness of the users' health. Some studies report that users complain about a headache, hand tremor and finger discomfort and pain of physical illnesses numbers increasing.

In fact, most mobile hand-held device users complain of discomfort at least on one area of upper extremities, back or neck.

Long –term usage of the device leads to additional tension on tenders , muscles and tissue etc. different kind of physical illnesses. Moreover, in research conducted by a group of Korean scientists from Inji University focused that an effect of cellphone on hand-held device users was a significant association between the total time spend using a mobile device each day and pain in the right shoulder, and between times spend internet browsing and pain at the base of the right thumb.

- The laptop and desktop negative influence

On the laptop and desktop negative influence aspect, although telecommuting and telework communication technology is popular to be applied to our daily life. For example, they are modern alternative to office arrangement, employees work from home office, café, garden, carpark , even car.

According to scientists showed that nowadays, there are 20 to 30 million people who work from their home at least one day each week. Another 15 to 20 million work when they are on the road, 10 to 20 million runs some form of home business and 15 to 20 million work at home part of the time. IN most cases, people use desktop and laptop in their home office.

However, modified cellphones or smartphones are also substitutes to a home office. In fact, in principle of computers, it makes the workplace safer and convenient to compare mobile phones. There are different examples of adaption desktop or laptop computers to health needs of these users when bring their computers to go to anywhere to use in common, e.g. ergonomically designed keyboards design, pad bolster, mouse etc. design to adapt to their carrying to use their laptop or desktop needs. However, laptop or desktop computer products have not proved any serious harmful to influence human health to compare mobile phones at this moment.

Consequently , although technology can create different kind of jobs to let human to do, or assist human to communicate conveniently, e.g. mobile or artificial intelligent robot assist human to do any clerical job duties or learning more easily, .e.g. internet or laptop or desktop or owning mobile and laptop function computer products. There high technological products can bring benefits to satisfy human needs, .e.g. raising productivity efficiencies for workers, providing far distance overseas phone calls telecommunication, searching data or electronic business running from internet channel. But human can not neglect that these high technological products whether will bring negative influence to our mental or physical health when we often use them in possible. Thus, often using high technologies products to influence our health issue will be one important matter to be our future consideration.

Artificial intelligence positive or negative influence

Will artificial intelligent technology cause war?

Nowadays, artificial intelligent technology is developed to be beneficial to bring positive impact to influence human's life. It is one kind of automatic machine learning to help human to seek the best solution to any problems by trial error to sure how the result is reached, it has computing power to learn any new skills, it is created artificial intelligence to own human mind to exceed ourselves human intelligence as well as the creation of new types of jobs. Such as non-manual driving automatic vehicles, insurance agents, investment analysts, and medical diagnostician etc. different trial error and mind analytical needs of characteristics jobs. Thus, it seems artificial intelligence will be possible to invent to the stage of own human mind. If their mind is bad, it is possible that which can dominate our life in the future.

Moreover, scientists predicted up to 50 % of today's jobs will be lost to these trends. Consequently, it will raise global unemployment number in the future. Thus, it seems that it will influence much human natural jobs are replaced by artificial intelligent job natural jobs in the future one day in possible. So, it means that (AI) can be perhaps to dominate human's mind and behavior in our daily life.

Thus, it also brings one challenge: Will (AI) threaten human's society to cause life danger if (AI) technology is applied to attack human to cause war by some countries' ambitious leaders. It is clear that this is a strange human's aim or intention to apply to (AI) technology, because it depends on what the (AI) manufacturers and/or inventors and/or the country's leader to consider being intelligent in the behavior of how they intend to apply (AI) technology in the future.

Thus, if any (AI) technology new discoveries are applied to assist employers to raise workers' productivities or performances and to help human to find error and trial and solve challenges. Then, it will bring benefits to human. Otherwise, of (AI) technology are applied to dominate human behaviors or minds or damage world peace. Then, it is possible that to bring technological war among ourselves. However, to achieve whom will be the leaders of our world's technological dominance. Thus, it is a horror technological war to influence our daily life in the future one day.

Reasons (AI) technology can bring negative influences

Why human will apply (AI) technology to contribute negative influences? What factors causes their negative behaviors? I shall give my opinions to support my prediction, judgement and uncertainty dominant of (AI) technology damage and to dominate to future human's societies that it is possible to occur.

Firstly, on artificial intelligent improvements in prediction (AI) technology and immoral decision making reason there is a risky action to scientists , whose payoff depends on a safe action with the same payoff in every application of situation. Judgement is costly, for each potential application, it requires thought on what the payoff might be. Prediction and judgement are complements as long as judgement is not too difficult. If some (AI) inventions are judged to make immoral decision to be applied in damage human safety aspect by scientists. Can we control it? It is the world's greatest opportunity and its greatest threat to encourage or attract the (AI) scientists to choose to do any technological damage behaviors to cause war occurrence indirectly.

It seems that mathematicians, philosophers, computer scientists and engineers who have responsibilities to spend their days thinking about how to avert catastrophes: meteor strikes, nuclear winter, environmental destruction, threats, when who attempt to apply (AI) technology to cause these damages to our earth.

There are a lot of things, that can go and have gone wrong throughout history, such as earthquakes and wars. But, these is one kind of thing that has not ever gone wrong. It is permanently destroyed the entire future by (AI) technology misuse. Thus, such as a man-made one: that rapidly advancing research into artificial intelligence might led to a runaway " superintelligence" which could threaten our survival. Whether countries' leaders will apply (AI) technology made machine men (machine soldiers) to become such as human soldiers to attack other countries in the future technological military war gaming. It means that if one day (AI) technological invention can implement to manufacture machine made soldiers successfully, then it can give chance to the ambitious countries' leaders to apply them to replace human soldiers to attack other countries. Then, the technological wars will be caused in possible in the future one day. Thus, scientists need to consider the future of defense to avoid artificial intelligent technology is controlled or dominated by the ambitious countries' leaders.

Against (AI) armed forces themselves. There are the active agents in terms of wetware (humans), hardware and software behind our efforts, generate defense and security efforts. Some scientists indicate the general artificial intelligent level had been improved to the artificial super intelligent level. Then, the technological war threats will be raised. Then, any countries' defense providers need to concern to predict when artificial super intelligence will achieve to this level to be caused technological war by (AI) artificial super machine soldier inventions.

The future of weaponized artificial intelligence

Why does it possible artificial intelligenc is weaponized? There are three key threat areas regarding of weaponized (AI):

- (AI) surveillance
- The (AI) weapons factory

- Careless destabilization of national security

Human future threat casting uses inputs from social science, technical research, cultural history, economics trends. We need to concern (AI) threat challenges, such as: Can we develop (AI) and rethink th very nture of (AI) without losing control over it? How to approach threatcasting and future modeling from an economic perspective? What will be the growth , impact and future of applying (AI) to real world industries?

(AI) threatcasting is a theoretical exercise undertaken by knowledge practitioners, such as (AI) scientists with special domain knowledge of how to specifically discrupt, mitigate, and recover from theoretical threat futures. Thus, (AI) threatcsting can be applied on technological military war problem. If human can predict when (AI) technology impacts to our lifes. We can predict when the future we want from (AI) technological achievement and the future we want to avoid from (AI) technologicl war.

What is (AI) weapons factory?

When one country has enough funding and the support to develop its most ambitious object to date, a super (AI) that could manage the world's energy and climat change. It is horror that it was actually building the world's largest (AI) weapons factory with the capability to invade every country in the region . Thus, it is only developed technological country, it has effort to invent (AI) super weapons to dominat or control overall world. If it aims to apply (AI) technology to give welfares to help human to solve challenges, e.g. climat change, seeking shortage enery. It is a good matter. Otherwise, if it aims to apply (AI) technology to dominate human's life safety. It is not a good matter. Thus, scientists need to avoid to do immoral behaviors to build (AI) weapons factory.

What is (AI) weapons?

In our future, now scientists will apply traditional (AI) technologies to manufacture (AI) weapons. Experience with traditional weapons allow organizations to understand the immediate mortal threat. (AI) weaponry shifts armament into more difficult to track, more integrated and systematically impactful.

This, is not only applies to individuals , but also to systems on an unprecedented scale. Imagine the destruction of an entire city energy system or the turning of common household connected devices (internet of things) into actors. As (AI) continues to be integrated into everyday tasks as well as into core everyday tasks as well as into core functionalities of cities and governments, the potential for turncoat or altered (AI) rises, increasing the potential for integrated (AI) threat actors operating behind the scences.

Thus, the weaponization of (AI) presents a new challenge as we imagine the changing nature of factories where software , instead of hardwares are created the crime have challenged how organizations defend and protect themselves. The coming weapons factories of (AI) will present a whole ethical, legislative and security issues concerning.

How to define and locate (AI) weapons factories? I feel the (AI) factories are no longer solely buildings , but a mix of vitual and substantially different facilities. Particularly as it shifts from a physical assemly and development model to a distributed and flexible networks. Needing minimal raw materials to develop weapons, the physical location of these factories could be anywhere and their identification from the outside, nearly impossible. To conclude for both benefits and threats, the integration of (AI) will impact the vast majority of human, changing how we interact, work and live. It means (AI) weapons are one kind of high technologicl internet skillful threat to our daily life. Thus, we need to consider hoe internet development to avoid netgative influence to our lifes.

If (AI) artificial intelligent digital systems are invented, when we use this new (AI) technology, we need o aware these questions to avoid (AI) digital systems threats. Such as how your personal data is being used and the implications , both positive and negative of sharing data. Demand that brand and organizations practice are inform you of how they are using your data. Awareness with populations and communities without access to training or education about (AI) safely. Explore the creation of an international organization that can oversee the development of (AI) to ensure that it is not weaponized.

Why (AI) technology will be dangerous?

We need to know technology is not science. Scientists are perceived as middle-aged, emotionally impaired and dangerous human. Science tells us how to the world is . That we are not at the centre of the universe is neither good nor bad, nor is the possibility that genes can influence our intelligence or our behavior. Dangers and ethical issues only when science is applied as technology . However, ethical issues can arise an actually doing the scientific research. Thus, it ws imaginative trial and error, such as (AI) technology that carries with it ethical issues from motor cars to polluting the environment and (AI) technology weapons of war in possible.

Some which the nucler was obtained. It seems scientists also do any hurt natural life behaviors to achieve experimental successful aim. Such as (AI) technological invention can be either beneficial or harmful to human's safety if who decided to profitability aim.

In conclusion, artificial intelligence is weaponized, it is possible to cause, it depends on the (AI) scientists to choose how to implement their (AI) scientifical research mission . Considerately, when general (AI) technology will be developed to reach super (AI) technology stage, human's life safety will be also threatened by super (AI) technology. Thus, (AI) scientists need to concern their behaviors whether are moral.

Planetary defense of space exploration war

Will space attacks be caused by advanced extraterrestrials?

I shall assume UFO, alien will attack human with logical extension where possible if human continue to concentrate on attempting to communicate alien. It is my opinion that possibility, however, small or large of such an attack exists from the simple fact that there are numerous other star systems in addition to ours.

The possibility of extra-terrestrial life is, withut a doubt, finite. Human is perhaps ignorant to believe Earth to be the only celestial body with a lifeform somewhat similar to our own. Whether or not the nonzero probability is large or small is of course unknown through scientifically verifiable and widely accepted evidence. However, the probability is finite. This being the case, it is also likely that if these aliens exists, some of them might wish use harm in some fashion or other for resons known only to them.

In fact, one UK famous space scientists had indicated that it is possible to influence some aliens to feel angry if human still spend time and nervous to attempt to apply space communication technology to connect them. His opinion implies human would be the natives is attacked by alien. The human race is to be considered as one civilization with multiple factions within it. Thus, he believes aliens this tims are coming , we must assume if one day, we can contact to aliens by space communication toolds successfully. Then, aliens will attempt to attack us if they dislike our contact and find where we are living in universe.

Thus, we need to develop a defense strategy for human civilization. For example, new space inventions need to be used to predict when space rocks will fly to damage our earth in possible. Hence, we have time to attempt to apply different space defense methods to avoid these space rocks attack to our earth to cause human death suddenly. Even, I feel space rocks are flying to our earth and human and aliens space communication contract which have close relationship. Hence, human ought avoid to continue to attempt to find aliens existence. It would be too late at that point to have much of a bartering position if the aliens could simply take what they wanted. Thus, aliens attack is not perhaps a science image or story, it is possible to occur in future one day. They probably would have defeated or inferior or super weapons to prepare to attack human.

We need to prepare is that we do not know whether or not we are alone in the universe. If we are the only intelligent lifeform, an interesting question relative to our existence arises. Are we an accident? Are we the result of an experiment? Thus, whether there are other intelligent lifeform in the universe, it is valid argument for a single species universe, but the science is weak and won't be discussed.

To conclusion, we ought defens of alien attck and ought not encourage space war occurrence, so we ought avoid to apply space communication tools to attempt to contact alien. We ought concentrate on exploring any undiscovered space resources to supply to human to use because our earth natural resources will be all used in future one day. It is possible that other planets will have water, wind, air, nuclear energy, gas, oil etc, undiscovered natural resources existence. Thus space scientists ought attempt yo invent fast speed of rockets, .e.g. nuclear power rocket to reach any planets to carry on researching any space undiscovered natural resources to supply to human to use because our earth natural resources will have shortage or not enought to supply to human to use in future one day. Thus, I believe seeking alien existence is not one important mission nowadays becaue it won't one beneficial attribution to human, but it is possible one harmful event to threaten our life. Thus, I hope space scientists need to consider whether seeking alien existence mission is value to continue to investigate.

Military operations in space

Nowadays, human is carrying on researching much space science. For space science, like nuclear science and all technology has no conscience of its own. Whether it will becom a force for good or ill depends on human scientists' choices as decisions. Whether this new ocean will be a sea of peace or a new terrifying theater of war from space undiscovered natural resources sources. I do say that space can be explored and without is encourage to cause space resource wars among different space explored countries during their space exploration stages. Countries leaders need to know that space superiority is th future of human resource welfares. We can not win a war without contrlling which country is the final dominance of space resource owner. Thus, space explored countries need to co-operate to achieve to explore space undiscovered resources successfully.

Today, space-based systems enable precision navigation provide real-time wether data, make possible global communications, gather intelligence and conduct surveillance. Thus, United States will be the leader to encourage different space exploration countries cooperation to achieve to find undiscovered natural resouces to attribute to humans to use, discourage to win whom will be the first space resource owner. However, US should continue to enjoy an advantage in space capabilities across all mission areas. This advantage will be maintained by staying at least one technology generation ahead of any foreign or commercial space power. The department will continue to develop responsive space capabilities in order to keep access to space reliable and secure. Survivability of space capabilities will be assured by improving space situational awareness and protection, and through other space control measures.

In fact, different countries have launch military space systems. Such as French military space program, it has placed remote sensing and electronic intelligence, gathering and communications satellites into space. Russians have had a comprehensive military space program. Thus, human needs have space law treaties to determine the extent to which they may limit military space opertations. It concludes with a dicussion of the appliability of humanitarian law to war in space, and to those aspects moe likely to come into play during any such conflict.

The nature of military space operations

Nowadays, space offers unique advantages to the war fighter. However, at least in principle, from space there is no point on the earth's surface or in the air space lying above it that is from space observation. Should space -based weapons be developed the same exposure would apply to earth-based targets.

What will be space weapons? Although few states posses the capability to attack satellites directly when space-borne, the ground-based systems and facilities on which they rely may be targeted to neutralize them, either through classic kinetic attack or information attack, such as computer netwok attack. Of course, signals to and from satellites may be jammed , altered, or monitored.

US joint (i.e. all military services) doctrine categorizes military space activities into one of four " mission areas", space control, space force enhancement, space force applicaton and space support. Space control includes combat, combat support and combat service support operations to ensure freedom of action in space for the US. Space military control missions ensure US government or space organizations have ccess to space and that the enemy doesn't. They encompass such activities as monitoring space, protecting friendly space-based systems and preventing the adversary's use of space for detrimental purposes.

Thus, space weapons are the war fighter's situational awareness or directly contributing to ground , sea, or air operations. Joint doctine subdivides force enhancement into five general categories: intelligence, surveillance and reconnaissance, integrated tactical warning and attack assessment, environment monitoring communications and positions, velocity time and navigation. For example, integrated tactical warning and attack assessment refer to detection of enemy activity or unclear determination, where as environmental monitoring encompasses collection of data on meteorological, oceanographic and space environmental factors of relevance to military operations.

Thus, space -based communications are the key weapon to effective network-centric welfare, in which friendly forces leverage information technology to operate synergistically. The final category ,position, velocity time and navigation employs space-based systems to boost the effectiveness of non-space based military operations , particularly precisin in attacks.

In conclusion, in the future human's space weapons will be high technological communication system, they can be applied to steal enemy countries' secrets or important confident data from governments or private organizations easily in possible. It will be relate to computer systems and super internet systems to manufacture any space weapon sources.

Will space exploration raise Mars wars crisis?

Any discussion of human exploration of Mars must begin with a description of the reasons why this planetary destination is chosen. It is possible that Mars planet owns undiscovered natural resources to supply human to use or it will be human's another earth to be suitable to live. Thus, it brings this question: Why does Mars have wars to be caused?

To answer this question, we need to believe that human hopes space tourism across the planet to warn a human colony that was the target. If human can prove Mars is another earth to provide places to let human to live. It means that many countries will hope to let whose citizen to fly to Mars , such as another colony to live. Thus, space colony exploration and competition will occur, due to Mars land and resource is limited, it can not provide all resources to let all earth human to live if human can prove it is one suitable planet for human to live.

It implies Mars will be only another destination to provide to humen to live in our future, instead of earth. So, Mars responds to a fundamental need in all of us. There is a human dream to explore. People must explore because they are human beings with a desire to expand the scope of human experience. So, Mars exploration adds to our knowledge , satisfies our curiosity and responds to our sense of adventure. Will Mars be another colony planet to provide to human to live? It is one influential event to cause different space exploration countries to prepare to dominate or own or manage this planet to live in our future. So, it is possible to cause Mars war among earth humans.

Why will exploration of Mars cause war?

Exploration of Mars is benefits to human , when scientists can prove Mars is one suitable living planet to allow human to live, or it has undiscovered natural resources to provide it to bring war among us during exploration of Mars procedures, favored a phased exploration approach , with a space station and lunar base preceding a human mission to Mars. I shall indicate the reasons that

will be caused war from exploration of Mars, such as below :
Firstly, if it is fact, Mars is proved a suitable planet to provide human to alive. Then, it is possible that many country leaders hope to emigrate their countries citizen to live to Mars, even they had not participated any exploration of Mars activities. For example, India and China both countries, which have high population and it had been increasing every year fast. I believe they also hope their citizen can attempt to emigrate to Mars to live also on day. However, it is possible that Mars is only one suitable planet to be discovered to provide human to live till to now. If future many earth people hope to live to this planet, but Mars has no many lands to allow houses to be built to provide to human to live at the same time suddenly. Thus, it cause one challenge of limit lands to supply to build houses to let earth human to live.
Then, what will be happened between countries by the fact of Mars is suitable to human to live ? I believe argument will cause between countries, due to Mars is one another earth to be suitable to provide to us to live. However, the goals of human exploration of Mars reappeared within the aerospace community, primarily due to the work of a small group of space enthusiasts that become known as the " Mars underground". When Mars is proved that it is possible another earth to be suitable to provide to human to live. It is fear that it will cause the ambitious countries, e.g. North Korean , because it owns nuclear bomb weapon to use it to be attack tool to attack other countries due to it dislikes other countries' citizens who can emigrate to Mars to live in future one day in possible, even, US developed country will be threaten by its nuclear weapon. Moreover , the high population countries, such as China and India , they will also be threaten to let their citizens to emigrate to Mars to live easily. Thus, it seems exploration of Mars countries, such as US needs to consider the nuclear war manufacturing countries, such as Korea. Its future Mars living threat, when Mars planet is proved that it is only one suitable planet to provide human to live in the future one day.

How to avoid space war occurrence?

Scientists ought consider space technologies' aim is only for protecting our earth's environment and managing its resources. Hence they have responsibility to deliver this message to let the ambitious owning space exploration countries to change their intention to attack human to achieve their dominance of space exploration owning aim. Because when the ambitious owning space exploration countries, such as North Koreans, when it feel it won't have any beneficial space exploration achievement or attribution from the space exploration country, such as US, then it is possible that it will choose to apply its nuclear weapon to attack US , even any other countries to threaten global human's life safety. Then the other countries , special the high population countries, such as China and India , they must have much needs to hope US can help them to apply air rockets to catch many of their citizens to leave earth to fly to Mars to emigrate to live if Mars can prove that it is one suitable planet to provide human to live. But, due to North Korean can not get any benefits from Mars exploration success. So, it will bring North Korean's nuclear bomb threat, it can influence their citizen to emigrate to Mars to live easily. Otherwise, if North Korean felt it can get any space exploration benefits, then it is possible that it will change its mind to cooperate with US to choose to manufacture nuclear energy power to assist it to push space rockets to raise its flying speed and raise enough nuclear energy power technique to supply any US's space rockets to fly to Mars during future any one of Mars journey. Then, the chance of space technology or nuclear war occurrences will be decreased. Even, Us space exploration country can gain North Korean's assistance to develop any further space exploration missions, such as Moon, Mars etc. space exploration missions more successfully and easily. Thus, high technological space exploration cooperation is the only one soluble method to avoid the future space or nuclear war occurrence absolutely.

Computer technology brings Nuclear or biological disease war

North nuclear bomb continue manufacturing threat

Nowadays, on positive hand, moral scientists had been inventing nuclear or biological technology which can be applied to manufacture nuclear energy power to raise space rocket's speed to be fast push and use less nuclear energy to prepare have enough energy to save to fly more long time, special is from the earth flying to Mars planet long distance, also biological science can be applied to DNA biological technology to be incent to attempt to attack cancer cells or other diseases to any patients in medical treatment in possible. But on negative hand, immoral scientists'
nuclear technology can be applied to manufacture nuclear bomb weapons to attack human, such as North Korean bomb invention weapons. Thus, it means that it is possible that North Korean had have effort to manufacture real nuclear weapons to attack other countries in future one day in possible. Even, North Korean had have effort to apply biological technology to manufacture disease to attack patient or health peoples' bodies to cause disease war in possible. Hence, we are facing nuclear war and disease war threats and we need to plan how to fight future North Korean's nuclear weapon or/and disease weapon attacks in future one day in possible.

Thus, if US can change North Korean's manufacturing nuclear weapon goal and to stop it's further nuclear weapon manufacturing to change to nuclear power manufacturing as well as it can also change North Korean's manufacturing disease weapon goal and to stop it's further disease weapon manufacturing to change to biological health medical medicine invention. I believe it can reduce the chance of nuclear war and/or disease war occurrences. So, it bring this question: How to persuade North Korean to stop to manufacture nuclear bombs and diseases to threat human's life safety?

I believe that if US can response to North Korean to give any space exploration benefits and biological medical medicine manufacturing techniques to this country, then North Korean scientists will be persuaded to change its mind to manufacture nuclear energy power and biological medical medicine products in possible.

I assume that US scientists had proved Mars is a suitable planet to provide to human to live as well as it had proved there are much undiscovered natural resource existence. Thus, US can assist North Korean scientists to help any desired to live Mars citizens to fly to Mars to live and it can provide the free charge of undiscovered Mars natural resources to satisfy North Korean peoples' needs to use. Due to North Korean want to get these Mars exploration benefits, the condition is that North Korean scientists need to stop to continue to attempt to manufacture nuclear bombs and they need to cooperate with US to manufacture nuclear energy to assist US space rockets to provide enough nuclear energy to fly to Mars more fast. I also assume that US scientists response to North Korean that it will attribute its any future biological medical medicine to North Korean to be free charge to use. Bases on the condition, it must stop to invent any diseases to attack human. Then , I believe that it has chance that North Korean will choose to stop to continue any nuclear bombs and disease manufacturing. So, US needs to forgive any future possible its Mars space exploration benefits and biological medical medicine invention to attribution them to satisfy North Korean's needs, if US wants world peace and we won't be threatened form North Korean's nuclear war and disease war in future one day.

Consequently, in this case, the humanitarian effects are sufficient to be considered unaccepted, such as between US and North Korean unfriend relationship, but it is hoped that this shading avoids confusion between the different scales of nuclear weapons and disease weapons are being discussed.

Explaining nuclear war and disease war negative effect as well as biological medical medicine and nuclear energy power positive advantages to let North Korean know

On nuclear bombs manufacturing and disease invention negative influence hand, US needs to explain to let North Korean to know that what is the negative effect if nuclear bombs are manufactured or undiscovered diseases are invented in success to cause nuclear war occurrence. The negative consequence will include: These nuclear bombs and diseases invention will influence the global environment to be poor, e.g. food shortage, water and air pollution, natural resource shortage, any creation of life, e.g. animal and human will be influenced to cause many illness, even death by nuclear pollution. Human will raise death chance due to any new or undiscovered diseases contact from air or water and to cause different kind of illnesses attack to our health bodies if air plans were catching any disease bombs or/and nuclear bombs to throw to any countries. Then, all earth human all will be killed on one day in possible. It is too horror matter.

The scientific reports are needed to suggest to let North Korean to know that , even a limited nuclear war would cause , apart from the millions of people directly killed, billions of people form starve from hunger because the resulting climate change would have catastrophic effects on global agriculture. The scientific assertion that any use of nuclear weapons would have catastrophic humanitarian and environmental pollution consequences. It aims to let North Korean to feel that nuclear bomb or disease bomb weapons will threaten both itself and other countries' people life safety.

On nuclear energy power manufacturing and biological medical medicine invention hand, Us needs to explain to North Korean to let it believes that owning technology to know how to manufacture nuclear bombs or to invent any undiscovered new disease which are not represent its' success and it has world leadership or dominant effort. It is foolish behavior and commit suicide behavior to North Korean itself. Because nuclear bomb and undiscovered new disease invention will cause North Korean all people can not survive in possible and all North Korean people survival chance be zero if nuclear and/or disease wars occurred. Hence, if North Korean scientists can change their opinions to stop to continue to manufacture nuclear bombs or invent undiscovered new diseases as well as to co-operate with US to attempt to manufacture nuclear energy power and biological medical medicine to supply to US to contribute to global human to use in medical science and space navigation and energy supply three aspects. Then, North Korean the country leader only him to get unlimited advantages, such as North Korean leader can free charge to catch space rockets to fly to Mars or Moon to travel, even he can live in Mars and uses unlimited Mars undiscovered natural resources to provide himself to satisfy his needs, even, he can get free charge to get undiscovered health medical medicines to avoid any cancel or undiscovered illnesses threats to cause his death. Selfish is the North Korean leader's aim, when he believes that it is only him to get these benefits if he can choose to stop to manufacture any nuclear bombs and to manufacture nuclear energy power as well as to stop to invent any undiscovered new diseases and to invent any undiscovered new medical medicines to treat cancers or death illnesses. Then, I believe that he will change his attitude from world dominance to world cooperation finally. So, US leader needs to indicate these benefits to let North Korean to understand why who needs to manufacture nuclear energy power and biological medical medicines clearly , such as below:

● Nuclear energy is the only clean, safe reliable and competitive of ensuring the continuation of North Korean industrial civilization when protecting its natural environment. It can replace a significant part of the fossil fuels, (coals, oil and gas which massively pollute the atmosphere and contribute to the greenhouse effect.) So, he ought not choose to continue to manufacture nuclear bombs.

● If the climate change and the end of oil, he must promote the more efficient use of energy, and he must use renewable energies, wind and solar whenever possible and adapt a more sustainable life style. But this won't be nearly enough to slow the accumulation of atmospheric CO_2, and satisfy the needs of North Korean itself industrial civilization and the aspirations of the developing nations. Nuclear energy power should be deployed rapidly to replace coals, oil and gas in the industrial countries, such as North Korean.

Korean ought concentrate on manufacturing nuclear energy power to assist itself industries development in the future.

● If North Korean chose to invent nuclear energy power, it will have these benefits to itself. Because nuclear energy power is an intelligent combination of energy conservation and renewable energies for local low-intensity application , and nuclear energy for base-load electricity production is the only viable way for North Korean for the future. Tomorrow's North Korean nuclear electric power plant will also provide power for electric vehicles for cleaner transportation to North Korean itself with the new high temperature reactors. Thus, North Korean will be able to recover fresh water from the sea and support hydrogen production for North Korean itself benefits.

IN conclusion, US has responsibility to explain why nuclear energy power manufacturing and biological medical medicine undiscovered new medical invention will bring much beneficial influences more than nuclear bombs and disease bombs manufacturing to impact North Korean future social development and economic development to bring positive advantages to itself. Moreover, US has also responsibility to control artificial intelligence negative development during it reaches the super artificial intelligence development stage to avoid artificial intelligence machines to manage or dominate human's societies or behaviors or cause super artificial intelligence factories negative global data information theft crisis of artificial intelligence technological war occurrence. Finally, it has also responsibility to persuade space exploration countries to consider their intentions are only space exploration contribution to benefits , it is not intention to achieve whom can dominate future space resources exploration to earn the country itself benefits. If US wants to avoid any future space war occurrence because themselves arguments concern whether whom own the final space resource exploration authority.

Consequently, the most important consideration is that space and nuclear and biological medicine and artificial intelligent scientists need to know that whose immoral behaviors will threaten human life's safety, include themselves. Thus, these scientists ought not only consider what future benefits who can earn to sell their inventions to the immoral businessmen. They ought consider how to attribute their inventions to satisfy human's needs and solve our challenges.

Future internet function development trend

● Online television

Online television channels, platforms, devices experiences and choice will be positioning entertainment consumer market for the foreseeabl future. The reason is onlin ebook, music entertainment has been popular. Why does online television won't be popular?

Bloomberg business week website (2013) indicated that the evaluation of control technological development of portability technological tool: from 1975 year , the astraltune product had been populaar. The, 1979 year, Sony walkman had reached the 200 million sold number. Next, 1994 year, the smartphone had reached 1.4 billion users. Following 2001 year, the Apple ipod had reached 350 million sold. Then, 2010 year, the Apple ipod had reached 100 million sold. However, in watching television/movie entertainment consumption consumers could have different choice, e.g. from 1975 year, consumers can choose VCR entertainment tapes to watch movies or television programs. Then, from 1995 year, consumers can choose DVD , following from 2007 year consumers can choose Netflix streaming recording cameras to record any movies or television programs to watch. It had reached 30 million subscription numbers. Following from 2012 year, entertainment consumers can choose Acreo FM internet signal to watch TV.

Anyway, the entertainment watching facilities development had been following this trend: Capacity from 1981 year, the capacity is broadband. then, from 1999 year, capacity is WiFi, it had 61% of households share market. Next, from 2001 year, the capacity is 3G technology, many people like to download any movies or TV programes to mobile phone to watch. Till to nowadays, the mobile phone capacity is improved to 4G technology, the mobile phone internet user number had reached 59 million current subscribers.

So, it implies that many entertainment consumers like to use internet to download any movies or TV programs to mobile phones or laptops to watch.

It implies future internet development trend which can be used to entertainment industry. Hence, the future of television ought have implications for the component of a media company, when it applies internet technology to operate, such as IT service management, disaster recovery, digital content security, cloud etc. technological development.

Interactive advertising bureau (2013) indicated the devices used to view online television among US digital video viewers by type Mar 2013 1% of respondent(s), laptp had 58%, internet-connected TV had 47%, desktop has 39%, smartphone had 28%, tablet had 28% , ipodtouch had 14%.

Hence, it implied many entertainment consumers prefer to use laptop or internet connected to watch online TV television or movie in the future. These two channels will be the most popular online TV/movie entertainment channels in the future. Moreover, future internet technology development ought concentrate on improving it's speed, quality, performance to satisfy any laptop or internet connect TV entertainment consumers. Hence, future internet technology development ought concentrate on improving it's speed, quality, performance to satisfy any laptop or internet connect TV entertainment consumers.

● Internet innovative logistic industry

What is future potential benefits and limitations of using internet to logistic operaters? The users pay attention to two new developments that may have a very large impact on the development of logistic has been pointed out, i.e. To the " internet of everything" and to the so-called fourth industrial revolution. Will internet be popular used by logistic transportation industry?

Nowadays, logistic transportation industry is facing challenges, factors include possibly quickest onset of transportation action, high efficiency as well as flexibility, whose main function is the maximinal adaptation to client needs, e.g. delivering any products or documents to any countries' clients in the most time and no any error to deliver the products or documents to the wrong receivers. However, internet is increasingly influenced by the skillful management of modern technologies to assist delivering in efficiency. It is based on complex and comprehensive data sources, arising from and influencing the development of modern trends. So, logistic industry needs have internet technology to help modern production, processing and logistics processes to satisfy the expectations of stakeholders.

The internet of things (IOT) is a new modes of communication, information connection between people and things, but in particular connection between objects (things). Hence, IOT management systems have a very wide range of applications and in terms of logistics, in a direct or in direct way many cover, among other, smart cities, intelligent industry, intelligent enterprises, intelligent buildings.

In the future, the group of significant trends in logistics include: big data/open data, cloud logistics; autonomous logistics, 3D printing, robotics and automation; internet of things; localization and local intelligence; wearable technology;augmented reality; low-cost sensor technology; crypto-currencies and crypto-payment. Hence, future logistics industry will need internet technology assistance to develop any businesses. For example, DHL logistic delivering firm, the first 6 trends belong to a group that will impact on : Firstly, big data/open data, it is a degree of digitization enterprise data can be shared in an unprecedented way. Integrated data streams in the supply chain of many logistic suppliers and open data sources have a very high potential for logistics operations, improvement of operational efficiency, full control over the suppl chain, assets and personal , the possibility of more accurate forecasts, and adjustment in real time.

Secondly, what is cloud logistics? It meets the challenges of complex diistributed , uncertains less predictable logistic conditions, reduction of the total cost of IT services (including the cost of installation, updatin , maintenance fees)., service risk minimization, faster and simply implementation, better reliability and security.

Thirdly, automonus logistic: It is stand-alone devices can be applied throughout. The supply chain from " the warehouse of the future" through auto-driven vehicles. Following the example of autopilots to unmanned supplies.

Fourthly, 3D printing is technology chnging the logistics by adding new manufacturing " mthods and possibl emergence of new market segments, such as the digital magazone.

Firthly, robotics and automation is the new generation of robots and automated solution will significantly better performance offers a serious alternative to manual labor, reducing time consuming actitivied aim. So, these will be internet is how applied to logistics industry trend in the future.

- Six key forces or " Drivers of change" impact on future internet development

In the future, there will have to key drivers of change impact on future internet development, it includes : the internet and the physical world, artificial intelligence, cyber threats, the internet economy, networks, standards and interoperability and role of government. However, thesedrivers will have three areas of impact include: digital divides, personal freedoms and rights and media and society.

However, future internet technology will have these threats to influence its development. They include: civil society is seen as more important to raise needs, internet must remain user centric to raise competition, it is critical for individual safety and for the future internet economy, new thinking , new approaches and new models are needed across the board from internet policy to addressing digital divides from security approaches to economic regulation, multi-stakeholder needs will change increasing frequenty, internet users wil consider data collection and privacy in confidence.

In the future, artifical intelligent development will incresse internet needs in possible. The advent of artificial intelligence (AI) promises new opportunities, ranging from new services and breakthroughs in science to the augmentation of human intelligence in digitial world. For example, when there is significant hype about the possibilities hat (AI) may bring voices of concern to apply internet technology assistance. Hence, human must ensure that humans remain in the " internet and (AI) driver's technology combination ."

Consequently, the hyperconnected internet economy that results will see traditionl industries to lead future new internet market leaders from around the globl driving innovation and entreprensurship. Hence, future internet and (AI) will be technological driven economy, it depends on how scientists improve their innovation.

However, scientists ethical consideration will be one important issue when they decide how to apply internet and (AI) technology. If they choose to apply them to war aspect, it is very horror matter to human's future safety. Hence, developing (AI) and internet technological countries need to consider scientist's behaviors in order to avoid war occurrence to cause human's death in future one day.

Hence, scientists ought follow this direction to develop internet technology. The future internet is needed to promise social development , economic prosperity and technologies that can ampify the best of humanity. But, it also brings about to solve challenges and questions to achieve to aim to raise human's social welfare or beneficial final direction.

What will be the certain factors to shape the future of the internet development? It includes as below: Social economic opportunity factor, it refers this ability how to connect people is essential to the internet's value as a platform for innovation, creativity and economic opportunity. How can the drivers of change encompass internet technological , economic, regulatory, security and network related challenges for the future internet . The drivers of change may include, such as how the internet economy development, what the role of government is, what the internet and physical world will shape, how internet assists artificial intelligent development, how to fight cyber threats, how networks standards and interoperable developments.

Future hospital, transportation, manufacturing etc. industries development factor how these industries develop, it will influence how internet needs. Because the rapid change will disrupt businesses and increse pressure on societies , particularly models and the nature of work will be profoundly changed to influence internet change needs. It is far from clear whether this internet technology driven assistance will favour existing internet platforms or bring greater competition and internet entrepreneurship.

How the internet economy will increase efficiencies, productivity and create new opportunities factor. Internet technology will reshape economies in ways stakeholders, and particularly governments may be ill-equipped to keep up with. And as technology drives automation, traditional jobs and the local economies that rely on them will be at risk. So, the future internet economy will depend on new approaches to skills and education. For example, traditional manufacturing sectors that were once relatively insulated must evolve to succeed in an increasingly connected internet economy. As devices and applicances are built to be network ready, the internet live needs us between manufacturing and manufacturing technological company increasing. Companies will need to adopt a technology mindset as they are from replacing parts to updating software to manufacture efficiently by internet and artificial intelligent technology assistance. Also, business is trying to protect against disruptions to their business models, for example, in the tussle between Google's automated cars and the automobile industry. For one, it's another application of sensor technology for the other , it's a change in mindset.

In the future, most widely used online services and platforms deeped their market position or face competition and possible displacement by new players? Could these internet companies face new competition from traditional industries as online in a world of IOT? Can internet platform be popular to be used for advertisements for businesses? (AI)/new generation of entrepreneurs like to use technology to solve local problems, reach global markets and drive innovation. Hence, online (internet) data search can be the best tool to help them to achieve their intention. I believe that it has not other technology can be replace internet to search lot of data in the short time within 10 years. Hence, internet of things (IOT) ought follo this direction to improve its quality to attract many clients. (entrepreneurs) to use this data serch service. Moreover, artificial intelligence will be popular to be used. It will be beneficial to internet to be used. For example, a society completely based on data collection on the business. Humans lose some self-determination through automated choices by connected machines. So, our community across all stakeholder groups and regions believes that automation generated through data analytics technology will have greater influence on human behavior and decision making. So (AI) and internet can be cooperate to assist themselves to serve human. For example, (AI) could bring about a fundmental reshaping of decision-making as policy development's increasingly data driven. AS (AI) and automation drive significant structural change across industries, the nature of work will change. Many existing jobs may be displaced as (AI) moves beyond user data to changing how products and services are delivered from internet assistance. The communication between machine to machine increases pressures to cut costs and people are being replaced. This is only going to increase with time. There are economic benefits , but also challenges to employees.

Hence, if the internet platforms of today can become dominant across infrastructure, services and applications, user choice and control over their online experience, as well as availability and deliversity of information and content could be popular factor to influence internet economy. When search companies reach such a level of scalability, it is difficult for others to complete with them. For example, customers may find it is difficult to move from one provider or platform to another. This will cause in the loss of choice

and constraints on innovation and lead to internet fragmentation. This is a trend to toward an ecosystem of users and developers, in which you can have the big winners or something similar to walled gardens. But there will always be some disruption tahta fragments this garden and creates a new paradigm. So , the reach and resources of internet platforms mean that startups will be acquired in their infancy, before they can disrupt the bigger players.
Will any internet companies replace Google, yahoo internet companies' services? This question is if smaller entrepreneurs are able to compare in an able to compete in an uncertain environment of investment analysis to the opportunities, these creates are ranging from new big data search service to the applied to intelligence in the digital world. So, artificial intelligence will be creative destruction. Many jobs will be also be eliminated by (AI) technological invention, but it can generate new jobs and jobs from internet , big data serch services assistance.

- Future trend of mobile and internet development

Morgn Stanley reserch indicated that future past mobile vs. desttop internet user development trend within 5 years. Mobile internet users number was from 400 million 2007 year climbed up to 1,900 million 2015 year. Otherwise, desktop internet users number was from 1,000 millon 2007 year climbed up to 1,7500 million 2015 year. Hence, it implied that , although desktop internet user number was more than mobile internet user number in 2007 yer, but till to 2015 year,mobile internet user number was more than desktop internet user number. It reflect many people had accepted to apply mobile tool to do any internet search behaviors. It is possible that it will be popular to apply mobile tool to do internet search behaviors for long time in the future.

It brings this interesting question: Why do global internet users prefer to spend more time to apply mobile tools to do search behaviors from internet? I shall indicate that this technological teaching method example, such as how smart mobile phones and internet technolgy had changed the old phenomena of learning model in educational industry. The traditional phenomena of learning model was that teaching innovation means unit cost of teaching, success teaching evidence means number of teaching units deployed, every student can free access open teaching contents from internet channel of desktop tools, every student learning can be achieved every delivery and display from internet learning, every teacher training needs to achieve the first and last discussion to every student from internet online teaching tool. Hence, many schools will accept to teach students from online teaching channel. Every student can turn on desktop to link to internet tool to learn at home conveniently. So, internet learning students do not need to go to schools, due to internet learning tool is similar to classroom to let teachers can apply internet channel to teach their students as well as students can listen their one teacher teach what in the same time when they open computer to link internet to see their teacher face and listen what who teach them after they log in their school website from internet channel conveniently. Hence, every group of students who can see teacher and listen what their teacher is teaching them in the same time after they turn on desktop to link to internet at home.

Some scientists also predict future mobie internet can be applied in educational and communication industries from 2020 year. Mobile internet can be applied to these aspects: education security, labguages, radio distributed systems, networking.

How can mobile internet be applied to children age education industry? I shall explain what what pocket school means. Pocketschool is not a name of device to be applied to different device for a different context, it is not a name software varies of open software contents, it is an initiative to help underrepresented children and migitate digital, education and economic divides. For a kind of mobile math learning game education method, it is a critical thinking math teaching method to children. Every child student can turn on mobile to learn how to apply simply math equation to calculation from mobile internet. Hence, future mobile internet tool won't only be applied to playing game aspect, it can be applied on education game aspect to let children to feel fun to learn from themselves. So, children can apply mobile internet to learn from device recognition to solve problem through collaborations, e.g. children cn apply moile internet tool to learn writting story ot telling story to increase learning internet or training to be authors. Mobile internet can also be applied to medical aspect, e.g. seeing any x ray images of brains , bones or any part of bodies, when medical photographs are delivered to download to the patient's mobile from the hospital easily.

In conclusion, in the future mobile internet will be popular used by mobile users and internet market must be expand to mobile tool market, instead of computer tool market.

- Digital Pollution prediction tool development

Can internet (digital) technology be fueled by the social, mobile, cloud, big data gathering and growing demand for anytime, anywhere access to information to help scientists to predict when or why or how any natural environment bad climate change occurrence and find any solutions to avoid any pollution is caused which can reach the serious level by human's damage natural environment behaviors?

Nowadays, the evolution of digital tool development, human can apply this tool to gather big data to help any businesses to decide to best activity to reduce loss, or to analyze information to get the more accurate result. In the future, I believe that digital technology can be applied to help scientist to gather nature climate and environment change data to analyze when the climate will be changed to be worse. Even, when water and /or air and/or soil and/ or noise different kinds of pollution will be serious to influence the country's people's health, e.g. water is polluted to drink or air is polluted to breathe or soil is polluted to grow food or noise is serious to influence our mental health. Even, digital big data can help scientists to find the reasons why the country's air and/or water and/or soil and/or noise pollution is caused and attempt to find any solutions more accurate to avoid the serious level of any pollution occurrence.

Moreover, in the micro –economic benefits, digital tool will develop to be used to predict the level of water/air/soil/noise pollution to assist policy decision makers to do any effective policies to response to these nature climate change challenges that cities face, include climate change and poverty, will be essential to making cities of the future competition.

Thus, digital technology seems to be future one kind of the most suitable climate change or environment pollution big data gathering predict tool to compare other climate change predict technological tools.

● Future digital technology prediction tool development trend

Nowadays, cloud, big data demand is growing to be satisfy to any different businesses or personal needs. In the future, it seems to be applied to help scientists to attempt to gather any big data to save to cloud (internet saving channel) , to analyze why ,when, how to cause the water/air/soil/noise pollution will reach the serious level and , to find the best solution to solve the causes of any pollutions accurately.

Digital technology will be one good prediction tool to help scientists, even who are not scientists to gather data to do any analyses concern climate change or environment pollution easily. It's advantage is any people who do not need to spend more time to learn and feel difficult to learn how to apply this technological tool to compare other difficult learning of technological climate prediction tools generally. Since, internet (digital) is one kind of popular and cheap technological product to be used, any people can free change to use it when who are using in public library , school library, any transportation tools, such as bus, ferry, tram, train, taxi private cars, or restaurant, shopping centers etc. different public places. Hence, gathering data activities are very convenient and easily to any people and it is one good prediction to predict when ,how, why natural environment change and climate change and pollution causes when people can bring whose laptops to go to anywhere to apply internet (digital) tool to gather any climate and environment data change immediately.

How can we use the internet tool to predict pollution to improve health

- What factors cause pollution?

Nowadays, pollution is global natural challenge. It affects the air we breathe, the food we eat, the places we live and the water we drink, which can cause a whole range of health issues. And it doesn't just affect humans. Pollution affects ecosystem of plants and animals, even global warmth crises.

Pollution is caused when something which has harmful or has poisonous effects is introduced into the environment. People and their environment can experience different types of pollution including: Soil, water, air, light, noise.

Firstly, soil pollution occurs when soil contains chemicals that are dangerous or toxic. Those substances put people in danger , for example, when they are exposed to high concentration of heavy metals in soils, as kit might lead to liver or kidney damage.

Secondly, water pollution is mostly caused by dumping industrial waste into the water bodies, spraying pesticides on plants or allowing detergents used for daily activities e.g. washing cloths into lakes or rivers. Water pollution not only harms the aquatic beings , but also travels up the food chain to us. For example, water borne diseases , such as typhoid or cholera spread mainly through polluted water either directly or through files or filth. It will cause water related diseases.

Thirdly, breathing polluted air puts people at a higher risk of cancer or asthma and other respiratory diseases. Coughing and wheezing are common symptoms experienced by people living in cities with high levels of air pollution.

Finally, noise pollution is caused by activities and can from traffic , airports, factories ,music concerts and others. People exposed to high noise level might suffer from sleep disturbance or hearing loss. It can also affect our mental health by causing stress or hypertension.

Hence, pollution damages the immune system, endocrine and reproductive systems as well as high levels of particle pollution have been associated with higher incidents of heart problems.

● Can internet be used to predict pollution?

No one really knows what the long-term effects some of these substances will have on the health of plants, animals and humans. As pollution is worsening around the world, technology and data collection methods are advancing which provides a great opportunity to understand and address pollution and related issues. It is important to know that pollution is a global problem, there are also lots of things, human can do as individuals and communities to reduce the amount we pollute as well as minimize how it affects us.

The internet of things can help us to do that by better manage health issues caused by pollution. I believe that our current technological development, it has not another technological tools ,which could be more suitable to replace internet (digital) technology to attempt to gather big data to predict climate or environment change factors to cause pollution more accurate, more fast speed, in the most short time ,more convenient in human's current technology development.

People around the world are already using the internet (digital)of things concept to tackle pollution mainly by installing various types of sensors that can measure quality of air or water. Data collected from the those sensors can provide an accurate picture of pollution levels in specific locations (for example, London city, UK ; New York and Washington cities, US ; Hong Kong city, China etc.) and that knowledge can help people better understand the issue and focus their efforts to solve the problems. There are also examples of how the internet of things monitor or/ and address health issues caused by pollution. Thus, there is a need for new ideas about how the internet of things can help us not only monitor , but also reduce , reverse and prevent the negative health issues caused by pollution.

If internet is really to help us to predict anywhere when serious level of pollution will reach, or why pollution causes, or how to solve pollution causes. Then, it brings these questions: What solutions are these of things enhance the amount of pollution we cause? How could the internet of things enhance these solutions? What existing internet of things solutions ? How could internet of things solutions help to prevent , reduce or monitor the impact of pollution on our health? How could internet of things solutions help raise awareness of pollution? How could it help people make choices that reduce the effect pollution on our health?

However, I believe that internet can be applied to assist doctors to predict patient's health condition to help themselves to make the accurate drug choice decision. For example, aerocrine has introduced a handheld breath to diagnose and manage asthma. The device can also tell a doctor the cloud can be used by doctors to analyze patient's treatment. Similarly, I believe that it can applied to help scientists to predict when and how and why any natural environment sudden change or climate sudden change to avoid our earth cause any kinds of pollution, e.g. air, water, soil, noise to reach the serious level to influence our health when any one is living in anywhere in our earth.

Currently, some scientists had invented new air pollution measure device and which needs to apply internet to gather big data analyses. Such as Buggy Air device is a project that is looking at how the internet of things can be used to measure air pollution at ground, or buggy level. Compact air quality monitors and GPD trackers can be fitted to a pushchair. The information collected can then be used by parents to avoid places at times , when these is high pollution. It could also be used to support campaigning . Thus, since internet can be applied to gather data to decide what kinds of drug are suitable to provide to the patient to eat on the medical aspect. Similarly, it seems that it can be also applied to poor climate change and poor environment change prediction aspect to predict when, how and why which concerns the different kinds of pollution will reach the serious level as well as to prepare to find the best method to help scientists to avoid our earth is polluted seriously.

How does internet predict air pollution

- Air pollution data analysis using time series method

Nowadays, the growth of technology and industries has made the life style easier, but adversely affecting the environmental conditions. Air pollution is one of the major global issues which needs to be resolved. The huge volume of pollution data collected needs to be understood and analyzed.

The time series pollution data can be used to extract patterns (seasonal) or novel pattern by techniques like clustering, prediction or forecasting, segmentation etc. large web serves and supercomputer clusters is an integrated part of future internet technology, which defines a dynamic global network infrastructure with self configuring capabilities based on interoperable communication protocols.

The internet of things consists of complex data types which includes sensors data, radio frequency data, video data and image data. The data can be categorized as: radio frequency identification data stream, descriptive data, positional data, environmental and sensor data etc. vast amounts of data are generated by the environmental sensors. The major challenge is to manage, analyze and mining data in its environment.

Air pollution is the major health issue affecting the urban areas of developing and the developed countries. These pollutants are also deposited on the soil, plants and in the water. This is a very critical issue nowadays, as it affects the population in different aspects , such as health, natural disaster etc. How to apply internet technique to understand and analyze the huge volume of time series pollution data? It includes these steps as below:

First step, data mining is the process of analyzing and knowledge discovery from a massive set of data. The major objective of data mining is to find efficient patterns from the huge volume of data received from the internet of things devices (sensors). Knowledge discovers pattern analysis is the main tasks of data mining for it. In city governance data mining is used to discover public need and decision making with automated systems improved service performance. The data mining techniques like classification, clustering and time series analysis used to solve problems in their area. For smart cities , city incident information management system can integrate data mining techniques to provide a comprehensive assessment of the impact of natural disasters on the agriculture.

Second step, classification techniques are used to predict a certain outcome based on a given input parameters. The classification methods , like decision tree can be used to classify whether a particular region is polluted or not . Based on the pollutant value, thus scientists can classify whether a region comes under the pollution categories like highly risky, risky, moderate and healthy. Data mining categories can be for policy making to manage the pollution. The classification and regression tree techniques uses specialized software to identify air quality with pollution levels. They (big data mining gathering) are then used to predict the future, pollution level based on the air quality parameters.

Third step, data mining clustering groups data set into subsets in such a manner that similar type of data is grouped together, when different data set belongs to different groups, clustering techniques like K-means and hierarchical clustering are used to determine the city cluster which are highly polluted. These techniques use a distance clustering are used to determine the city cluster which are highly polluted.

● The challenges of data mining

Although, internet technology can help scientists to gather big data in short time anywhere. However, the data mining gathering process will have these challenges to cause to threaten their tasks. So, scientists need to spend time to attempt to solve data mining in order to achieve the most efficient and high performance and the most accurate results for their every time population level analysis. The challenges of data mining include as below:

- Data mining algorithm challenge involves selection of a suitable data mining algorithm to handle huge volume of data. Selectin of data mining model challenge includes how to manage and analyze massive set of data generated. It is necessary to select an efficient data mining model.
- Accessing and data extraction challenge is as a large volume of data. Data extraction and accessing is a major challenge. Handling of heterogeneous data challenge is the feature of data in environment gathered from different sensors and platforms. The challenge is how to handle these heterogeneous data and to analyze.
- Data storage challenge is as a complex task to store and retrieve huge volumes of data. Database management challenge is a research challenge in internet of things environment. How to selection of database management software and tools to handle big data to predict when or how or why the serious level of environment pollution reaching will occur, but it also have these challenges to be solved in order to achieve the most accurate research result.

In conclusion, nowadays, it is possible that only this artificial intelligent technology , which seems have effort to compare to internet (digital) technology to predict when, why, how poor environment change or poor climate change occurrence in the shorten time. Due to artificial intelligence will be invented to be applied to different aspects, such as assisting handicapped people to walk, auto-driving, moving cargos in warehouses, auto-cooking . Thus, it is perhaps that it can be applied to help scientists to predict when, how, why poor climate and poor environment changes which will reach the serious level of pollution to anywhere. However, internet (digital) technology is only one human's potential pollution prediction tool be applied to gather big data to predict pollution to get any result which is more accurate, more easier , more efficient , more convenient , to compare other technological tools. Hence, future environment scientists ought concentrate on researching how to solve internet (digital) data mining gathering challenges in order to apply this internet technology to get the more accurate pollution prediction results for health issue. Thus, how to raise internet efficiency and performance to gather data mining challenges will be urgent matter to let environment scientists to solve to achieve to carry on researching any pollution issues to everywhere in our earth to avoid serious level of pollution occurrence to influence our health in future one day.

CHAPTER FIVE

Factors influence Canada computer market development

and Norway Similar behavioral consumption model

Nowadays, Canada and Norway both countries have similar economic development models. I shall indicate what reasons to support my view point to believe that they have similar consumption model in their societies as below:

They have a strong trade and investment relationship are built on complementary resources, similar levels of development and shared interests and values. Hence, these both macro-economic and micro economic factors will influence Canada and Norway countries overall both social consumption models to be similar to influence themselves people (consumers) daily behavioral consumptions are more similar.

Because both Norway and Canada are advanced economies, basic trade is augmented by research and opportunities to help both countries deal with similar geography and climate. It causes Canada export or import success. Thus, Canada's trade success which will depend on Norway trade cooperation. Also, Norway's export to Canada will influence Canadian social consumption model to be similar to Norway's social consumption model as well as Canada's export to Norway will influence Norway social consumption model to be similar to Canada's social consumption model. For example,

Norway's investment in Canada supports Canadian GDP and jobs. In spite of the heavily materials, based outputs of both countries. The relationship makes a unique contribution to the knowledge and innovation economy.

In fact, Canadian and Norway people whose life habits are very similar. Moreover, Norway's impact on the Canadian economy includes on these aspect: Technology, telecommunications, utilities, consumer services, oil and gas and financials. It will influence Canadian general social consumption model after Norway consumption model on these Norway similar industries investment are brought to Canada to influence Canadian's daily life or life habitual changes to cause follow Norway people's consumption model or attitude in daily life. (Canadian Aquaculture Industry Alliance) indicated for example, agriculture is an important sector for the Canadian economy, providing jobs and investment in every province, as well as the Yukon.

The aquaculture sector employs over 8,000 Canadians, overwhelming in British Columbia, New Brunswicky and New foundland and Cabrador. It seems aquaculture sector is one factor to influence Canadian's behavioral consumption model.

Canada and Norway negotiated a path of closer trade relations through the Canada-European Free Trade Association (CEFTA) agreement in 2009. This could be strengthened through updated foreign investment protection and promotion rules, such as through a foreign investment promotion and protection agreement. Due to Canada and Norway have trade and investment relationship have trade and investment relationship. It will influence Canadian's life habits and consumption people's consumption model after Norway's business investment is introduced to Canada.

For example of Norway industries communication development to influence Canadian's consumption desire changes include as: Information and communication technology aspect; Canadian Trade Communication Service (2012) indicated that as a society, Norwegians are some of the top per capita users of information and communications technology (ICT) in the world, and they also have some of the highest spending per capita on ICT. Norway ranks sixth on the international telecommunication Union's ICT Development Index, which ranks countries' performance in terms of ICT infrastructure, use and skills. Norway is an advanced ICT country with related industries that are based on globally competitive.

Nowadays, ICT expertise has developed around the country's more traditional sectors like oil and gas, aquaculture and the shipping industry. However, it also has expertise in niche areas, such as food mobile banking solutions, micro payment and customer relationship management (CRM) technologies. Because of the ICT synergies, Ontario's technology corridor in South Western Ontario provides attractive investment options for Norwegian companies. Encompassing the greater Toronoto Area and Kitchener-Waterloo cities in Canada, this region is known for its high tasks expertise and entrepreneurial spirit. Hence, it seems Norway's communication industry development will influence some Canadians who live in Toronoto or Waterloo etc. large cities' consumption model to follow Northway people's consumption model in mobile cell useful time, habitual usage mobile phone calls, e.g. average 100 hours increase to 200 hours or more per month, due to cheap mobile phone call charge factor; long distance phone call increasing time to use, due to cheap distance phone call charge factor; food consumption channel on internet ecommerce shopping consumption model.

Canadians also often use internet to see movies, listen music or reading or searching information etc. different entertainment aim at homes, due to cheap internet charges to home internet users. Hence, after Norway communication industry is invested to develop in Canada, it will possible to cause many Canadian change their behavioral consumption model in Canada communication industry consumption market.

- Living standard, productivity and competitiveness to international comparison factor

Why does living standard, productivity and competitiveness to international comparison factor influence Canadians' behavioral consumption change model? What is productivity mean? Productivity measures the efficiency with which production inputs, such as labor and capital are being used in an economy to produce a given level of output. The key determinants of productivity include" the education, training and experience, the workers and the the amount and types of equipment available to them, as well as technological innovation and changes in both organizational and management practices.

In this view point, these determinants are influenced by broader factors, such as competition openness market. The term " competitiveness" means as a measure of a country's advantages or disadvantages in selling its products or services in international market. Hence, Canadian's consumption behaviors will be influenced by how it's products are produced as well as its competitiveness with internationals, which are interconnected that contribute to strong Canada's economic growth and rising living standards. For example, in the year, if Canada's productivity effort is raised and export or import number is more than last year, its domestic Canadian who are living to cause who have more jobs to do. Then, they have more effort to consume, due to their living standards are risen in this year, who need to consume anything to satisfy whose better living of standard demand.

Another example, I assume that the more efficiently Canadian businesses use resources to produce products and service in this year. That is the more productive, they are the greater their advantage in selling those products and services in international markets, that is the most competition, they will be. Then, Canadian will have more different kinds of products to choose to buy from local manufacturers' products supply. The more product choices influence will bring many Canadian choose to buy local products more than overseas foreign import products. The reasons are possible what local products are cheaper than foreign import products, local products have much different kinds of unique choice, more than foreign similar kinds of products. It will have more local different kinds of product choices will influence.

The trend of buying desires to Canadian's consumption is to be changed foreign manufacturing product import who will trend to choose to buy Canadian's domestic manufacturing products in the year. Hence, Canadian's manufacturing more different kind of unique product choice will influence Canadian who desire to buy foreign manufacturing import products to change to desire to buy Canada domestic manufacturing products, due to they can provide more different kinds of products choice to sell to them in this year. Past, they can not buy many of any these Canadian domestic manufacturing products traditionally. Consequently, in the year, raising productivity and raising living standard and raising competitive effort factor will influence Canadians change their behavioral consumption model in this year.

When these high technological products can be manufactured more number and sell more in Canada after future ten years. then, these high technological products can sell cheaper price, due to Canada's artificial intelligent manufacturing skill has reach the mature stage. Hence, Canada artificial intelligent scientists can innovate high qualify and low cost material to manufacturing kind of artificial intelligent robots in order to sell more number and reasonable cheap price for this kind of (AI) research and development high technological products after future ten years research and development process. Consequently, it will influence future Canada (AI) home consumers acceptance to choose to buy any kinds of (AI) robots to assist housewives to share their home workload for Canadian families in popular after future ten years. Moreover, future Canada (AI) robot products will be also popular to use for different functions for any businessmen, e.g. shopping center (AI) robot cleaning service, houses or offices or any building (AI) robot cleaning service; restaurant (AI) robot cooker's cooking service replaces to human cookers. (AI) non-manual automatic transportation vehicle send products to deliver to different places; (AI) robots deliver product to suitable locations in warehouses.

Hence, future after ten years, when Canada innovate to research (AI) robots technology to be success. Then (AI) robots will be popular to be used to Canada domestic some (AI) users and business (AI) users both. Canadian's consumption model will be accepted to high technological (AI) consumption model as well as innovation will influence future Canadian how to choose to apply high technological product, such as (AI) robots will be used to replace human general job duties in office or home or business function to replace themselves tasks for main consumption intention in future their daily high (AI) technological innovation life trend model.

● Innovation policy factor influences Canadian behavioral consumption model

How can Canada policy decision makers innovate Canada social consumption model? Nowadays, Canada policy makers are giving increasing attention to innovation. Innovation strategies are being designed in more countries. International policy learning or innovation related issues becomes an important tool for industrial policy development. To answer above question, I shall ask whether it has relationship between innovation and consumption desire in any countries.

Such as Canada innovation case, the economic structure of Sweden and Canada differ with respect to e.g. industrial structure, where the Canadian industry is more characterized by small businesses when Sweden's industry is dominated by way large and international companies. These structural functions have very strong impacts or national innovation policies and strategies that lead to different solutions, which offer valuable prototypes for learning.

However, both countries are have similarities as well as differences between them. They are facing a growth challenges, Sweden needs to increase both the number of start-ups and growing companies, when Canada's environment strength seems to close to US, its foremost competition and also its biggest export market. The economic structure of Sweden and Canada differ with respect to e.g. industrial structure, where the Canadian industry is more characterized by small business when Sweden's industry is dominated by international companies.

The importance for small businesses of a measure corresponds to the correlation between the function of the measure and the circumstances for the targeted group in Canada. Canada innovation policy achieves to small business target group, e.g. integrated business, technology advice, which implies a network of people with different competences, but easily assess through a low number of entry points. The efficiency in the use of public research and development resources is related to the approach to commercialization of results in science and research in universities and research institutes that are publicity funded or owned.

Hence, in micro economy view point, Canada government innovate technology to assist many small business development, it will encourage many small business target group businesses to attempt to enter themselves local sale market in Canada. Then, there are many small businesses exist in Canada, it can influence Canada consumers have much different similar kinds of product choice to buy in anywhere easily and conveniently. The advantages are some consumers who do not need to drive cars to go to very far distance to their homes to buy cheap or expensive products because there are many small business stores provide different similar kind of products to let them buy more easily and conveniently. Consequently, it will influence many Canada consumers‘ consumption desires to be risen , due to who do not need to drive cars to anywhere to buy, who can choose to walk to buy any different kinds of similar products in short time.

Hence, innovation policy can encourage way small businesses set up to cause some Canadian who live far from large cities people, whose consumption desires are also influenced to be increased. The improved macro-economic situation has also made possible, e.g. strategies tax reduction, large increase in research and development expenditure, strengthened the venture capital sector and measures to increase highly qualifies labor through support for graduate university studies and improvements to Canada's immigration policies. These changes will also influence Canadian's behavioral consumption change model. For example, Canada innovation strategy related to education strategy and mainly industry and research and development policies. The focus on these four areas: Canada's knowledge performance skills, the innovation environment, and the need to strength the innovation capacity of communities. The strategy mainly focus on investment development on innovation issues on research and development, such as any technological industry development. Hence, after future ten years, Canada will be possible one high technological development country to follow US, UK, German etc. high technological development countries. In the future, when Canada's research and development success, some high technological products use be possible to be manufactured from Canada's manufacturers, e.g. any artificial intelligent products, non-manual driving vehicles, robots,.

- Immigrant economic and social factor influences Canadian consumption model changes

Canada immigrant brings Canada negative with the deterioration in economic outcomes, such as the changing mix of source regions and related issues, such as language and school quality, dealing returns to foreign experience and the deterioration in economic outcomes for all be labor market entrants of which immigrants are a special case. Due to immigrant brings negative influences to Canada's economy development, it will influence Canadian has negative consumption attitude, because economic downturn to cause Canadian domestic low education workers will lose jobs, due to foreign low educations Canada can pay cheaper wages to compare Canada domestic low educational workers. Hence, Canada's employers can choose to employ the low educational workers to replace domestic Canada low education workers. Then, it will cause many Canada low education workers unemployed and they will feel difficulty to find new jobs to do, due to they need to compete with foreign Canada immigrant job seekers.

Thus, long -term many Canadian low educational worker unemployment challenge will cause low consumption desire social challenge, and many Canada small businesses will lose these domestic Canadian low education consumers (target consumer group) to cause their businesses fails in possible. Hence, long-term serious many foreign low educational sudden immigrate to Canada, which will be possible to cause many low educational Canadian lose jobs to cause their consumption desire to be less consumption to buy any not essential products or not essential entertainment.

● High impact firms accelerate Canadian competitiveness influence technological product consumer behavioral changes

Many US technological products are exported to Canada to bring much weaker. Canadian domestic technological firms' technological product attractive effort, it reflects a competitiveness challenge for Canadian firms.

These US technological products are sold to Canada, it will also influence Canadian consumption model changing, such as the Canadian technological product consumers' habitually choices to buy any domestic manufacturing technological product, it is possible that are US technological products are imported to Canada market to increase different kinds of US high technological products for Canadian to choose to buy. They will influence the habitual Canadians who are traditional any Canadian high technological product consumers, who will change consumption model to choose to buy US different kind of technological product, even their prices are possible higher than Canadian high technological manufacturing products. It is possible that Canadian domestic high technological product manufacturers who can not manufacture any better functions or more safe or more beautiful or unique high technological products to compare US high technological product manufacturers.

Hence, although Canada can earn much imports income to raise GDP every year growth from US high technological product imports, but long term bulk of US high technological product imports, which will influence Canada domestic high technological product manufacturers' income to be reduced when they still choose to buy their products in local possible, due to they encounter US high technological product manufacturers' competitiveness every year. It implies Canada domestic high technological product manufacturers need to concern their consumer choices will increase and whether Canada is still their original market to sell their high technological products in the future.

Implementing Canada's rural development policy in a knowledge-driven economic consumption behaviors.

Nowadays, Canada government considers have to implement rural development to encourage consumption to raise economic growth. It aims to improve Canada's economic restructure and increase competitive effort in global, e.g. agriculture, forestry, mining and fishing sectors etc. However, Canada government will encounter these challenges to need to solve in order to implement its rural development strategy more easily. These challenges include resource depletion, substitution of synthetics for natural commodities, substitution of capital for labor in production, relocation of natural resource industries to low-cost jurisdictions in the developing world, and low level prices on global markets, which are no longer mitigated by subsidies, trade protection and business incentives.

What is knowledge-driven regional economic development mean? (like forestry, fishing, agri-business etc. , diversification of the rural economies through service industries and tourism, development of small and micro enterprises, exploitation of the potentials for search and development, selective infrastructure development and social development in especial better access to health care and education).

Why knowledge-driven rural development will encourage rural consumption to Canadian. There reasons include knowledge-driven manufacturing can influence Canada rural consumers to feel base fresh shopping feeling, it is different and better consumption model to compare traditional rural consumption model. For example, Canada rural development strategy is targeted at knowledge production exchange and commerce in rural consumption market. It involves entrepreneurs, researchers and venture capitalists within, for instance, the agri-business and bio -products, energy and agriculture. Thus, Canada rural business development will have possible to influence any rural favorable product consumers to raise whose desires to choose to buy any fresh idea or undiscovered rural products in this Canada rural consumption market.

● How can greening of the Canadian economy to influence businesses' behavioral changes

Will Canada economy development raise Canadian green environment consumption desires? to answer this question: we need to know what green consumption means, it can be explained to develop in a low carbon, resource-efficient social consumption desire. Canada needs to know why Canadian feel who needs environment consumption. The reasons include supporting environmental protection, innovating improved assurance criteria and methods to deepen enterprise responsiveness to the green economy agenda, motivating stakeholder engagement and the use of best practices and standards to give better understanding of the views and the actions of all those affected by the green economy, driving through leadership in the area od challenge and opportunities posed by the green economy through focused research and skills development.

Canada government also needs to know Canadian is facing a series of major environment and social challenges. Such as: the need to produce more food to feed growing populations; how to manage of competing demand global fresh water supplies; the significant and expanding challenges of climate changes. Thus, when Canada government lets Canadian to know why green environment protection rural consumption model will protect global environmental climate changes to avoid worse and our natural resources won't waste to use to cause shortage possibility. Thus, Canadian will change consumption behaviors to reduce waste to use. Canada government can promote climate change effects to let Canadian to know include: increased risks of extreme weather events, effects on infections disease dynamics, rising sea levels leading to rain of land and water sources.

Thus, such as how to protect earth environment and nature resource shortage issue, Canada government needs to promote it is human responsibility to reduce to waste to consume any resources. To let Canadian to reduce waste from their consumption behaviors. It is social education which concerns human, such as Canadian how to avoid waste from their traditional consumption behavioral model to change green environment protection consumption model in their daily life. Then, Canada will have much natural resource to supply for Canadian to use and Canada's natural environment will also keep clean, when Canadian feel need to change their waste consumption habitual behaviors for themselves in order to give benefits and welfares and raising green economic growth for themselves country.

● Increase productivity growth influences to increase social consumption in Canada

Canada's recent productivity performance is insufficient to ensure that future generations will enjoy the growth in incomes that current generations are accustomed to. The productivity growth influential factor includes the most important determinant of how increased material living standards; it is also critical to ensuring that adequate fiscal pressures associated with population aging. Thus, when Canada can increase productivity growth, then it will have enough products to supply to Canadian to consume. The question is how to raise productivity growth?

As its root, productivity growth is driven by innovation and investment in capital equipment and Canada is behind most other industrialized nations on both of these. With regard to innovation, sharp proposes expanding federal technology transfer programs that assist firms in exploiting best practice innovations. With regard to capital investment, sharp identifies high taxes at the main proposes abolition of sales tax on machinery and equipment, this tax advantage can give economic benefits to encourage Canada businesses entrepreneurs to invest businesses to do in Canada.

Thus, it can encourage business investment migration to bring Canada's productivity growth. However, the effect of productivity growth will be the only means to ensure not only the increasing living standards or increasing social consumption to which Canadians are accustomed, but also the resources needed to meet the fiscal pressures brought on by population aging, due to productivity growth must need more resources to be supplied to manufacture any products ensure.

Thus, if Canada expected consumption can be grown, it needs to solve resources shortage challenge to ensure it has any resources to supply to manufacturers to manufacture any products to cause productivity growth aim for long term macro economy development.How can greening of the Canadian economy to influence businesses' behavioral changes

What is greening economy mean? It can be defined to efforts to improve environmental conditions are motivated by government environmental policy, environmental and economic efficiency and corporate responsibility. Thus, apply this definition to Canada, we find a four step greening process that is common across all sectors of the economy. This process suggests that environmental considerations have become heavily influences into the behavior of Canadian firms.

What are characteristics influence how firms approach greening in Canada? For example, greening economy can influence unconventional oil and the mining businesses, we find that demand elasticity, collaboration and international trade considerations are shape greening efforts. A key finding is that environmental initiatives and economic growth are not alternatives, but rather increasingly can complement one another.

How does Canada greening economy influence Canadian

businesses' behavioral to be changed? The notion of the green economy and instead focus on the greening of the economy as a basis for assessing the progress being made by businesses and individuals to achieve economic growth with environmental benefits. There are several trends become apparent about the relationship between the environment and the economy in Canada. Such as: Canadian corporates are increasingly any environmental considerations into any decision making. Canadian cooperates consider how to improve environmental efficiency frequently results in cost advantages, how to raise incentives to reduce environmental impact which can be in strong driver of innovation and Canadian corporates consider corporate responsibility is a driver for improving environmental performance. Hence, Canada greening economy policy influences Canadian firms consider have to apply environmental protection methods to achieve any best advantages or benefits to themselves. However, Canada government has implemented to do more conservation, emissions, sustainability successfully. Otherwise, it ought consider how heightened environmental awareness is having a positive impact on environmental outcomes and highlight how green initiatives are increasingly complementing economic growth.

In fact, on the one hand, Canada has a resource-abundant modern industry economy. In the 1600 year to modern forestry , mining and oil and gas extraction, the development of the commodity sector has always played a key role in Canadian economic development and economic growth. So, these industries need many labor to serve to help them to develop their businesses in Canada, e.g. forestry, mining and oil and gas extraction need environment protection in order to achieve Canada natural environment to own enough natural resources to supply to them to produce any products, e.g. Canada needs have enough trees to provide woods to manufacture furniture, natural resources to be supplied to manufacture oil, gas etc. gas energy.

On the other hand, green jobs are necessary to Canadian greening businesses. Green jobs are jobs within industries and businesses that have a positive green impact or at least a significantly lower negative impact than their rival(s), which are most able to capitalize on the growing governmental , business and consumer desire to minimize and mitigate human's effect on the environment.

Consequently, Canada greening economy influences Canadian greening business considers how to raise greening labor individual skills. A green job is one whose predominant function serves one or bot of the following goals. Such as conserve energy or reduce pollution. This includes clean energy alternatives, products or services designed to conserve energy and other natural resources and efforts prevent reduce, control or measure environment damage. In effective, if Canada expected green economy success. It needs to encourage any Canadian related greening product sale businesses how to raise greening labors; skills and how to reduce pollution to keep natural environment more clean in order to achieve more natural resources have enough supply to let them to use to manufacture any products to sell to satisfy Canadian consumers' needs.

How growth strategy influences
Canadian consumption model changes

Canada government commits to deliver growing economy to a strong middle class consumer target group, such as social middle level income people, who are owning properties and vehicles etc. fixed assets in general. It aims to encourage this target consumer group to increase consumption desires, where then benefits of growth are shared in a fair and equitable manner in Canada's society today. Thus, it aims to encourage this Canadian middle class income target group's consumption desires in order to raise Canada economic growth.

It brings this question: How can Canada government encourage this middle class income target group to raise their consumption desires. It will encounter this macro and micro economic challenges to attract this middle class income target group's consumption desires. Such as Canadian households' high debt levels still represent a key risk to housing and consumer spending, especially if the economy were to face slower income growth. Moreover, increasing levels of household indebtedness and rapid increases in house prices in Canada's largest housing markets which will influence this middle class income consumers' consumption desires to be decreased.

However, Canada government had attempted to achieve these strategies to raise this middle class income target group's consumption desires. these strategies include as below:

(1) To foster greater innovation, the Government is creating innovation Canada, a new platform that will make it easier for Canadian innovators to access and benefit from Government led innovation programs. Supporting business led innovation which will facilitate collaboration between innovators and potential clients on research, development and demonstration activities that pursue major commercial opportunities, establishing a new strategies innovation fund will encourage and simplify existing business innovation programming and focus on attracting and supporting new high-quality business investments and launching the Pan-Canadian artificial intelligence strategy which aims to promote collaboration between Canada's main centers of expertise and position. Canada is as a world-leading destination for companies seeking to invest in artificial intelligence and innovation. In addition , the Government is established on invest in Canada Hub, new federal body dedicated to attracting leading global firms to Canada, in order to bring more jobs, fresh capital and new innovative technologies to the Canadian economy. Thus, it seems that Canada promote to artificial intelligent products market to attract middle class, even high class income people to feel that they have needs to buy any kind of (AI) products to use. Also, it encourage (AI) technology firms to set up in Canada in order to raise more (AI) related work chance to let them to work in order to raise high (AI) technological educational workers' income level to encourage them to consume in Canada domestic consumption market.

(2) To help the Canadian workforce acquire the job skills needed

to adopt and succeed to raise more employment chance to cause economic growth in order to raise social consumption desires of these three stages to achieve the final effect to raise social consumption desires. Hence, Canada government focuses on educational innovation aspect, it is expanding the labor market transfer agreement to increase the delivery of skills training and employment services aimed at helping Canadian find and maintain employment. It is also expanding the eligibility for Canada student loans and grants to make post-secondary education more afford for adults returning to school after spending several years in the workforce as well as part time students and students with dependent children.

It is the goal of the government to desire the best possible education outcomes for Canadian to raise whose knowledge level to prepare further to find jobs to work easily. Also, the government is making investment to support in increase in the number of high quality, affordable child care for low and modest income families to allow parents to pursue new opportunities to learn and to return to work. Hence, it is one long term education strategy to aim to raise Canadian knowledge or education level to achieve more Canadian can become the middle class income level consumers to encourage them to have effort to consume to raise economic growth to push economic development.

Consequently, Canada government's growth strategy aims to assist many Canadian have effort to become to be middle, even high income level target consumer group in order to encourage them have effort to raise consumption in Canada's society. It concentrates on implementing long term education and job skill upgrade level to young people as well as innovating high technological artificial intelligent products research development both aspects. Hence, growth strategy needs spend much time to raise long term education level and (AI) technological innovation level in order to achieve to encourage the middle level or high level income target consumers' consumption desires to be raised.

Reference

Canadian Trade Commissioner Service (2012), " Information and communications technology profile-Oslo-Norway" Government of Canada: Department of foreign affairs and international trade (Now Dept. of foreign affairs trade and development). June

Canadian Agriculture Industry Alliance: Economic benefits. http://www.acquaculture.ac/files/economic benefits. php

www.ingramcontent.com/pod-product-compliance
Ingram Content Group UK Ltd.
Pitfield, Milton Keynes, MK11 3LW, UK
UKHW041838190726
13854UKWH00002B/596